"The life journey of David and [...]
Acts, with the Spirit empoweri[...]
the joy of knowing Jesus in mu[...]
respectful and sustained dialogue with Muslims sets a high standard
for spiritually grounded witness in a world too often polarized."

—**J. NELSON KRAYBILL**, president of Mennonite World Conference

"'When he calls me, I will answer.' This was a popular chorus that
we sang in East Africa. Answering the call of God requires boldness.
David Shenk is quick to add that such boldness, however, is a gentle
kind. In this book, you will encounter exactly that gentleness as
David tells his story of responding to the Lord's summons to make
a difference in the world. My family in Kenya is an example of
those who were touched by this gentle yet bold response. From the
orchards of Lancaster County to East Africa and beyond, Shenk
tells stories of encounters as a peace witness to God's transforming
power. This is a must-read for those who believe in the difference
that Jesus makes! I heartily endorse it!"

—**NELSON OKANYA**, global missions president at the Center for Serving Leadership

"This book drips with the love of Jesus. The stories contained here
transport us to places and people we think can never be reconciled—and yet miracles happen! And all it takes is saying yes to the
call of Jesus. If you're looking for examples of how mission and
peacemaking go together or ways to be inspired in your own faith
journey, say yes to this book!"

—**MICHELE HERSHBERGER**, Bible and ministry professor and department chair at
Hesston College

"This lively memoir testifies to a remarkable journey of Christian
faithfulness that spans an astonishing range of continents, contexts,
and cultures. The sources of David Shenk's confident witness are
clear: a deep love for all of God's children, an unwavering focus on
Jesus, and an irrepressible sense of joy. The legacy of his work—
especially in Muslim-Christian relations—will echo for decades
to come."

—**JOHN D. ROTH**, professor of history, director of the Institute for the Study of Global
Anabaptism, and editor of the *Mennonite Quarterly Review* at Goshen College

"David Shenk is my friend and mentor. This memoir gifts us with stories from his childhood on through to the peak of his international and diverse career as an ambassador of Christ. Transcending memories, it tells a story of communities of faith impacting and interacting in surprising ways. The Mennonite church that sent David out to share Christ was itself transformed by discoveries of the Spirit by those to whom they witnessed. Beyond a missionary tale, this is a story of a missionary God who invited David along for the ride!"

—**JONATHAN BORNMAN**, member of the Christian-Muslim Relations Team at Eastern Mennonite Missions

"David Shenk's teaching and example have been foundational for my own life of mission and ministry, so I have eagerly awaited this book. In it, David uses his gifts of storytelling to give us a deeply personal account of the people, places, and contexts that have shaped his work. It's a story of the joyous adventure that awaits those who, like David and Grace, say yes to Jesus."

—**LORRI BENTCH**, mission team director for Eastern Mennonite Missions

"If you get weary in well-doing as I do, then listen to David Shenk, who insists: 'Let God surprise you.' Take it from a man who knelt in prayer as a small boy when the East African revival swept his hometown. Watch as he keeps saying yes even at unexpected, inconvenient, awkward times, in the presence of heads of state, witch doctors, Bible college students, church bishops, and imams. You will see and hear living proof that laying down one's life daily for Jesus promises joy-filled surprises, unexpected, divinely arranged adventures, and 'holy mischief' for the sake of God's reign."

—**REV. JIM LAVERTY**, lead pastor of Mountville (Pa.) Mennonite Church

"David Shenk's gentle and bold approach has set an example for a generation of interfaith peacemakers, now spread out across the globe. His invitation to the reader—let God surprise you—is evident even as he looks back over his own life of service in response to God's calling. Jesus met young David in Tanzania, sojourned with him in Somalia and onward, and now meets us on the pages of *A Gentle Boldness*."

—**PETER M. SENSENIG**, member of the Christian-Muslim Relations Team at Eastern Mennonite Missions

A Gentle Boldness

A Gentle Boldness

SHARING THE PEACE *of* JESUS
in a MULTI-FAITH WORLD

David W. Shenk

Harrisonburg, Virginia

Herald Press
PO Box 866, Harrisonburg, Virginia 22803
www.HeraldPress.com

Library of Congress Cataloging-in-Publication Data
Names: Shenk, David W., 1937- author.
Title: A gentle boldness : sharing the peace of Jesus in a multi-faith
   world / David W. Shenk.
Description: Harrisonburg, Virginia : Herald Press, 2021.
Identifiers: LCCN 2021017947 (print) | LCCN 2021017948 (ebook) | ISBN
   9781513801353 (paperback) | ISBN 9781513801360 (ebook)
Subjects: LCSH: Shenk, David W., 1937- | Mennonites--United
   States--Biography. | Peace--Religious aspects--Christianity. |
   Christianity and other religions. | LCGFT: Autobiographies.
Classification: LCC BX8143.S435 A3 2021 (print) | LCC BX8143.S435 (ebook)
   | DDC 261/.873--dc23
LC record available at https://lccn.loc.gov/2021017947
LC ebook record available at https://lccn.loc.gov/2021017948

A GENTLE BOLDNESS
© 2021 by Herald Press, Harrisonburg, Virginia 22803. 800-245-7894.
   All rights reserved.
Library of Congress Control Number: 2021017947
International Standard Book Number: 978-1-5138-0135-3 (paperback);
   978-1-5138-0136-0 (ebook)
Printed in United States of America

25 24 23 22 21   10 9 8 7 6 5 4 3 2 1

Dedicated to
J. Clyde Shenk,
my father,
who loved Jesus

In your hearts revere Christ as Lord.
Always be prepared to give an answer to everyone
who asks you to give the reason
for the hope that you have.
But do this with gentleness and respect.

1 Peter 3:15

Contents

Part V—The World: God's Grace All the Way (1980–2005)

Part VI—Christians and Muslims Engaging for Peace in Their Respective Ways (2005-2020)

Foreword

Several years ago, I attended a consultation on religious dialogue between Muslims and Christians hosted by the Mennonite church in Burkina Faso. David W. Shenk was one of the primary presenters. At a certain point in the gathering, David expressed interest in having an informal meeting with the local Muslim chiefs and other *ummah* leaders. As we gathered outside under a massive baobab tree next to the mosque in a nearby village, our delegation "gave the news" through translators, expressing gratitude for the hospitality we had been experiencing since our arrival.

The encounter lasted over an hour, with all participants sharing the joys and struggles they faced in their various communities. As the meeting drew to a close, David said, "As followers of Īsā al-Masīḥ—Jesus the Messiah—we are children of Abraham. And we are told that we are blessed in order to bless others. Would you be willing to receive our blessing for you in your life here in the village?" Our conversation partners seemed a bit surprised, yet were genuinely pleased with the offer. When the prayer-blessing was completed, David added, "Now, we know that you, too, are children of Abraham and are blessed for the purpose of blessing others. Would you consider extending to us a blessing as well?" The old village leader stood to his feet and, with hand gestures and a strong voice, uttered words of goodwill, health, peace, and safety on our behalf.

I have known David Shenk for many years. As a young Bible and church history teacher in Côte d'Ivoire, I put to good use his writings on world religions, peacemaking in African contexts, respectful interreligious dialogue, and Africa's vital contribution to Christian history. In more recent years, I have seen him captivate audiences in local congregations and international gatherings with endless stories from his life as a globe-trotting messenger of the Prince of Peace. I have spent countless hours with David coediting manuscripts in readiness for publication. I have enjoyed his company and wise counsel at the annual gatherings of the "Christmas Circle"—a small group of church leaders who have met for the past decade in fellowship at year's end. And in all these encounters, I have been the privileged recipient of David's gracious spirit, his unconditional and sometimes unmerited encouragement, his inexhaustible ideas, and his boundless energy.

David has faced his share of obstacles and discouragements along the way—the sudden and tragic deaths of his mother, Alta, and brother, Joseph; the cultural shock he experienced entering North America as an African-born son of missionaries; the early resistance he encountered to his mission style and understandings from more culturally conservative Mennonite church and mission leaders back in the "homeland" headquarters; the termination of fruitful ministries in Somalia; and moments of risk and danger when he voluntarily placed himself in vulnerable situations with unknown and unpredictable conversation partners.

But David is a tireless disciple of Jesus, endowed with an exuberant spirit and a seemingly bottomless supply of optimism and hope. Relying on God's Spirit and accompanied by Grace—his lifelong companion and faithful ministry partner—David has repeatedly turned roadblocks into opportunities and tragedy into triumph. No one embodies more fully one's own life motto, in David's case that of 1 Peter 3:15 (NIV 1984): "In your hearts, set apart Christ as Lord. Always be prepared to give an answer to everyone who asks you to give the reason for the hope that you have. But do this with gentleness and respect."

David has spent a lifetime, in a spirit of "gentle boldness," sharing the peace of Jesus in a conflicted world. This is David's story. And we need to hear it . . . in a world still dreadfully conflicted and still in desperate need of the peace of Christ.

—James R. Krabill
core adjunct professor at Anabaptist Mennonite
Biblical Seminary and coeditor with David Shenk
of *Jesus Matters* and *Anabaptists Meeting Muslims*

Preface

I was born in Shirati village in Tanganyika, East Africa, by the shores of Lake Victoria. My parents were Mennonite missionaries from Lancaster County, Pennsylvania, and they bore witness to Jesus and his peace among a people who had never before heard of Jesus. Bumangi was my boyhood home.

When I was a child my mother read Egermeier's *Bible Story Book* at bedtime. As a little boy of six I asked my parents this question: "What difference does Jesus make?"

The answer to that question is the reason I am a Christian. For eighty years I have asked that question day by day as I travel in the way with Jesus. I hear wherever I travel that Jesus is the principal peacemaker. Paul refers to his mission of peacemaking as ambassadorial peacemaking. By God's grace I have been appointed to serve as his ambassador for peace. I and my wife Grace have been investing our lives in this mission of serving as peacemakers for Jesus.

About three years ago Amy Gingerich, executive director of Herald Press, asked if I would be interested in writing a book on missions. She said, "We need a book that celebrates the joys and challenges of living as a people of peace. We need a book that encourages and inspires a joyous and exuberant commitment to Christ and his mission in our day."

I told her I would love to write that book.

She said, "Then go for it."

That invitation formed the seed of this book, a book that I hope "encourages and inspires a joyous and exuberant commitment to Christ and his mission in our day." The Anabaptist communities with whom I am most closely associated—Tanzania, Somalia, Kenya, Ethiopia, and the United States—form the core of the book, along with a wide diversity of stories, each a miracle because of how many people were touched through the years. The stories began one hundred years ago, when there were no Mennonite churches in the East Africa region, and today these churches comprise a million followers of Jesus. It's amazing how, from a small farming community in eastern Pennsylvania, seeds were planted that have brought a tremendous harvest.

This is a book of miracles.

This book celebrates the joy of communities of persons coming to faith in Jesus and bringing transformation to their homes, their communities, and their nations.

This book lends itself well to encouraging conversations of Jesus bringing about his kingdom in your own respective communities, discussing what is happening in your own home area.

As Grace and I have worked on this two-year effort we have sometimes shed tears of joy, and it is with enormous enthusiasm and hope that we share with you what we have heard and experienced in communities around the world.

As it says in Revelation 5:9, "You are worthy to take the scroll and to open its seals, because you were slain, and with your blood you purchased for God persons from every tribe and language and people and nation."

May this book encourage you to fulfill your part in bringing to fruition Christ's work in our day.

Introduction

Saying Yes

I was flying to Nepal when an unexpected email came through from the office of the president of Tanzania. I was traveling through Dodoma, the capital of Tanzania, as a global consultant for Eastern Mennonite Missions (EMM), working on a Swahili translation for my book *A Muslim and a Christian in Dialogue*. It was a five-year process.

In any case, it was during this time that I received an email from the president of Tanzania, who had become interested in the work we were doing with that very book.

"The president has heard you are in town and is delighted that *A Muslim and a Christian in Dialogue* is now available. He would like you to stop into his cabinet room before you leave town. Your meeting with the president has been scheduled." The email went on to explain the date and time of the meeting, where to go, and what to expect on arrival. It turned out, the president was eager to speak with me about Muslim-Christian relations and to encourage a path forward where both groups could continue to live in harmony in Tanzania.

We were surprised and grateful for this invitation by the president of Tanzania. But my itinerary during that trip to the region was completely full. I glanced over the days, the people I was to meet and the places I was to go, and I simply had no extra time slot to meet with the president. I would have to decline.

I wrote back with my apologies (in hindsight I do wonder, how could I be so dense?), saying thanks but no thanks. I couldn't come. My schedule was full. Maybe another time. I closed my computer. I convinced myself the opportunity would come around again.

I have to wonder how many times, as Christians, this is our response to the call of Christ, when that still small voice speaks. How many times does Jesus himself come calling, asking us to do something, to say something, to go somewhere, and we are quick to point out the busyness of our schedules, the many burdens on our time? How many times do we politely refuse Christ? What if we committed to begin accepting these invitations?

This is a book about saying "Yes."

Very soon after my reply to the office of the president of Tanzania, I received another succinct email from them. I could tell by the tone that they were not used to being told "No." The message was simple and to the point.

"When the president says come, you come."

Fair enough.

So as soon as I landed in Nepal, I told my hosts, "We'll have to meet another day. I'm going to see the president of

Tanzania." And I got back on a different flight and returned for my meeting with the president.

After going through security, my wife Grace and I were ushered into a waiting room outside the council chambers of Tanzania where the president held important meetings. Others waited there as well, and we were called in one at a time. Later, we would discover that the president broke out of a cabinet meeting to make time to meet with us.

He came into the room, greeted us, and we sat around the table together. "I'm extremely excited about this book on Muslim-Christian dialogue," he said. "Christians and Muslims simply do not understand each other."

He went on to say that he would like a large number of books, all of which he would pay for himself. "I think that might be a bit many," I said, taken aback by the number. "Perhaps we should start with half that?"

Bishop Amos Muhagachi (middle) and I (left) presenting *A Muslim and a Christian in Dialogue* in Swahili to Jikaya Kikwete, former president of Tanzania, 2011.

He was very concerned that every Christian and Muslim leader in Tanzania have a copy.

In addition to ordering the books, he wanted me to host a meeting between all the key Christian and Muslim leaders of Tanzania, a dialogue that he hoped would open up a way of peace between the two groups. I was asked to plan it and steer it, along with Tanzania's Mennonite bishop Amos Muhagachi and Steven Mang'ana.

These meetings took place a few months after he called me to his office, when we had an unprecedented seminar for Muslims and Christians in Tanzania. I ran it alongside my Ugandan friend and Muslim coauthor of *A Muslim and a Christian in Dialogue,* Badru Kateregga.

I remember one of the first things we said as we greeted the attendees: "All the children of Abraham are to bless all the people of the world. This is God's command in the Torah, is it not?" There was a lot of nodding and murmured replies in the affirmative.

"Okay, well, you are all children of Abraham. Are you making people joyful and blessed as you relate with them?"

What followed was a wonderful, spirited conversation about how each group was blessing the world, as described by the other group. So, Muslims listed the ways that Christians were blessing the world, and Christians listed the ways Muslims were blessing the world. It was a tremendous conversation.

On the second day of our two days together, the roof nearly blew in spirited contention. The conflict was in response to comments made by my partner, Badru, who urged that Tanzania become a member of the Organisation of Islamic Cooperation. Divine intervention and the wise leadership of the Muslim and Christian co-moderators finally got us back on track.

The conflict revealed the apprehension felt by both Christians and Muslims regarding faith in the political order. Christians prefer the Tanzanian secular state while the Muslims yearn for an Islamic state. The tensions that surfaced revealed the need for regular dialogue, and as a result, I was invited to help facilitate similar local dialogues at the town and village level.

There were seeds of peace sown that day in ways that I never could have planned or imagined, were it not for the invitation I received and (eventually) said yes to.

If, indeed, when the president of a nation calls, the response must be "Yes!", then how much more should our answer be "Yes" when Jesus calls! How much more eagerly should we lay down our responsibilities and previous engagements, and follow Jesus into the calling where he would like to lead us?

Again and again, throughout my life, I have heard that call, for I have been appointed by Jesus to be his emissary. I will always be amazed that Jesus chose me for ambassadorial service. Sometimes the Holy Spirit has a great plan, yet no one is listening. The summons from Jesus comes in different ways, through different people—you might, as you listen to the call of Christ, be as surprised to hear the call as I was.

I am writing this memoir as an encouragement to you: listen to Jesus, and reply to his call with an unreserved "Yes!"

The stories in this book are accounts of Jesus calling and sending ambassadors to the ends of the Earth. It is a calling we must not ignore.

But there were other seeds sown as well, decades before that day, and we bore witness to the fruit of those long-ago planted seeds after we left the president's office and stood at an immigration desk going through departure formalities. The officer glanced at me, glanced at Grace, looked back down at our passports, and asked us an interesting question.

"I see from your passport that you were born in Shirati, Tanzania," he said to me. "The Mennonites who live in Tanzania are from Shirati. Are you perchance a Mennonite?"

"Indeed," I replied with a smile. "I am a Mennonite Christian, born in Shirati."

"We Mennonites love Jesus. And we like to sing about Jesus. May I sing a song for you?" So, right there in the immigration line, Grace and I were serenaded by a fellow Mennonite Christian. He sang two songs of praise to Jesus, and the passengers in the queue were delighted.

How could it happen that a Tanzanian immigration officer in Dar es Salaam (a name that means Place of Peace) would cross our path, tell us he is a Mennonite as well, and bless us with hymns in his native Swahili?

This book describes the amazing answer to that question.

Part I

Tanzania: The Seeds of Faith
(1933–1952)

1

The God Who Went Away

Eighty years ago, in an apple stand in Lancaster, Pennsylvania, Central Market, on a market day that might have seemed like any other, a woman named Emma called over to her son, J. Clyde.

"There he is, Clyde," Emma said. "Go and ask the preacher your question."

Earlier that week, Clyde had confided to his parents that he believed God was calling him into missionary service in Africa. His father, David, openly wept as his only son described this inclination that God might be calling him to leave the family farm and move overseas. Emma had wisely encouraged her son to share the calling with their pastor, Jacob Hess, the next time they saw him.

The opportunity came in a busy farmer's market stall. Clyde motioned for the pastor and led him into a side aisle.

"Pastor Jacob," he asked earnestly. "Should I go to Africa as a missionary?"

What a question.

At that time, a small missionary team from Lancaster was blooming in Tanganyika, a sovereign state that made up the modern-day part of mainland Tanzania. In 1933, Eastern Mennonite Missions took action to seek an area in Africa where the gospel was not known. Several weeks before Clyde asked his pastor to confirm his calling, a train was chartered for 475 passengers to carry well-wishers from Lancaster to New York City, for a grand farewell at the dock, seeing off the first Mennonite missionaries to East Africa. Fervor for mission among Mennonites, essentially a peasant farming community, was a response to revivalism that swept through their congregations across North America at the end of the nineteenth century.

One of the seeds of these Mennonite revivals occurred in 1896, with a tragic train and buggy accident just north of Smoketown, Pennsylvania. Enos Barge and his fiancée were killed on a foggy evening after coming home from a party of young people, and their death spoke powerfully to the young people who, up until that time, were rarely baptized until after they were married. After that accident in Lancaster County many young people repented and were baptized, and for some of them this revival also meant a recommitment to the mission of the church.

But this conviction for mission didn't begin in the nineteenth century. It was formed within the Mennonite movement in Germany, as well as the Swiss and Dutch wings of the early Anabaptist movement, as far back as 1525, when sixty Anabaptist leaders met in Augsburg to plan for the evangelization of the world as they knew it. Their favorite preaching text was the great commission of Matthew 28:18-20, yet most who met

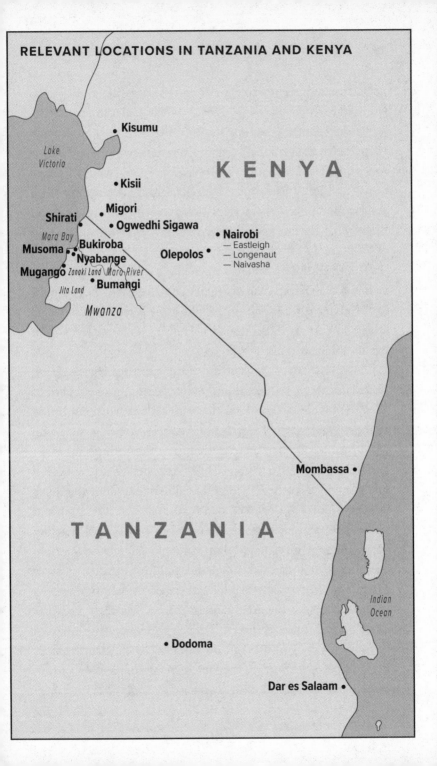

RELEVANT LOCATIONS IN TANZANIA AND KENYA

Lake Victoria

Kisumu

K E N Y A

Kisii

Migori

Shirati

Ogwedhi Sigawa

Mara Bay

Nairobi
— Eastleigh
— Longenaut
— Naivasha

Musoma

Bukiroba

Nyabange

Olepolos

Mugango

Zanaki Land

Mara River

Bumangi

Jita Land

Mwanza

Mombassa

T A N Z A N I A

Indian Ocean

Dodoma

Dar es Salaam

in that missions gathering were martyred within three years. Consequently they became known as "the quiet in the land."

By the sixteenth century, European church life had become united with the political system. Christians who believed that following Jesus in a politically centered way went in directions that didn't harmonize with Jesus and his teachings. The state system opposed practices such as adult baptism, a central practice of the burgeoning Anabaptist community, and that was the center of the persecution.

The freedoms of America opened the doors to rekindle the vision for mission that characterized the early Anabaptists in the sixteenth century. As a child I knew we were a people whose history included martyrs. That legacy ran deep within Mennonite spirituality.

However, it was only in my church history classes many years later that I learned about the sixteenth century refusal of Mennonites to participate in the wars against Muslims. It was in those classes that I learned of Michael Sattler, a man who would rather die as a martyr than join the European armies and kill Muslims for whom Christ had died. Many followed his example, a costly decision that led to martyrdom and being labeled traitors against Christendom.

Mission and peacemaking have always belonged together in Anabaptist missiology! For example, an eleven-year-old boy, John Mellinger, who later became president of Eastern Mennonite Missions, asked his father why Mennonite pastors seemed to ignore the great commission of Matthew 28. That question was used of the Holy Spirit to expand the stirrings of interest in missions. And on my desk is the *Dordrecdcht Confession of Faith* from the Dutch Mennonites, published in 1632. This seventeenth-century document calls on all believers to proclaim Jesus as Savior and Lord and to take the gospel to those who are not believers.

So it is that these Anabaptist traditions have made their way through the centuries. Four hundred years later, Sattler's love for Muslims would reappear in my own heart.

The inquisitive conversation in the aisle at Central Market that Clyde had with his pastor was happening among Mennonites throughout North America as a response to the movements of the Holy Spirit at that time.

Revival meetings sometimes packed out the meetinghouses. One service was so filled with repentant believers that a young man's only option was to walk atop the benches in order to come forward for the prayer of confession. The youth culture at the time was very much formed by revivalist preaching, since many young people attended church on Sunday evenings for the social and spiritual development. My grandfather was so affected by the revivals that he discontinued raising tobacco and turned his fields into orchards.

These revivals often grew, spilling over into tent meetings, such as the George Brunk tent meetings of the 1950s. Thousands attended, and when an invitation was given to accept Jesus, people flowed to the front of the assembly by the hundreds for prayer and confession.

Bishops sometimes fretted that the renewals were developing a new kind of Mennonite. Indeed mission and renewal were happening, sometimes in spite of objections from conservative bishops.

Jesus was calling, and people were responding with an unhesitating, "Yes!"

My father, deeply embedded in this culture of revival, leaned into Jesus' call, but he experienced no such objections from his own Mennonite pastor, who with quiet command took in his lanky, six-foot frame, leaned in and said, "Young man, let the Lord have his way." The simplicity of this response moves me, even to this day.

That young man, J. Clyde Shenk, the one earnestly seeking God's call on his life, eventually became my father, and his "Yes" to the invitation of Christ shaped my life forever.

My father left that meeting with his Mennonite pastor in Lancaster's Central Market and shared his growing conviction with his fiancée, Alta Barge, who was also experiencing a call for missionary work in Africa. The struggle to confirm this calling was intense, and it wore on my father as he engaged with God. He lost sleep, his appetite, and thirty pounds as the days passed. He didn't want to leave his father alone to run the farm; yet he had heard the call. How could he say no?

He imagined entering this life of deprivation: there would be no tomato soup; he assumed he would have no John Deere tractor at his disposal, as he did on the home farm. Nevertheless, within two years my parents were in Tanganyika.

But my father's conversation with his pastor didn't happen in a vacuum, and unbeknownst to him, there were larger movements going on at that time that would support Jesus' call on his life. Businessman Orie Miller, the general secretary of Eastern Mennonite Missions, along with the board, had taken action in 1930 to move forward in mission, in spite of strong resistance. During one board meeting, the treasurer cautioned the group: they could commit $9.62 to missions in Africa, obviously much less than what would be required.

Orie expressed his conviction that the funds always follow the vision.

A year later Orie Miller and farmer Elam Stauffer set out to explore where the Mennonites of Lancaster Conference would open their first mission. The Holy Spirit led them to London for consultation with missions leaders, then on to Berlin. Wherever they went their hosts prayed when they arrived in an office and prayed when they left—that much praying was quite strange to these Mennonites.

They traveled to the border of Sudan, but Orie's international commitments meant they didn't have time to enter the country, so they caught another boat south and arrived in Dar es Salaam—yes, the same Dar es Salaam where, decades later, Grace and I would be serenaded by a Mennonite customs official.

Wherever they asked for advice, locals consistently encouraged the Mennonites to consider the Musoma District on the shores of Lake Victoria. That region had some eighteen small language groups, and the larger mission agencies had remained focused on larger language groups. Here was a need the Mennonite missionaries could hope to address.

It is interesting to me to reflect on how all of these events happened almost simultaneously, how my father's individual calling was confirmed by his pastor during the same general time period that Orie Miller was working to prepare the way for the arrival of missionaries in Tanganyika, and specifically the Musoma District. The serendipity of these events, taking place without corroboration between the various parties, serves as a reminder to me that I do not have to be overly concerned with how my calling will play out in the larger context of the world; my primary concern must simply be saying "Yes" and taking the next step laid out in front of me.

When Orie Miller and Elam Stauffer arrived in Mwanza on the lakeshore, they met a man called Praying Shoes. He was Emil Saiwalka, a member of the Defenseless Mennonite Church in Indiana, serving with the Africa Inland Mission. His name came from the fact that his shoes turned up at the front, for he invested many hours on his knees in prayer. Emil and Elam marveled at how the Lord had orchestrated these plans, bringing two Mennonite leaders from so far away. Knowing that Elam was in good hands, Orie departed for appointments in India. Emil and Elam rode bicycles for 150 miles across Musoma District, exploring the region, searching for an ideal place for the Mennonites to begin their East Africa mission.

When the two men arrived at Shirati on the lakeshore, Emil assured Elam they had found their place. Later, on the first Sunday, twelve people convened, and the local chief was even in attendance to welcome the guests. Yet Elam was concerned: there were a large variety of wild animals, and humans were few and far between. Emil assured Elam that those who were interested would carve out homesteads and begin clustering near the great tree on the hilltop, Katuru Hill. That is exactly what happened.

When the first permanent missionaries arrived at Katuru Hill, they were eager to get going. After all, they had come all this way to bear witness to Jesus. Even though the barriers were great, they tried to tell the story of Jesus with Swahili, Luo, Kuria, English, Arabic, Zanaki, and other languages. They explained to the native people that they were believers in God.

The Africans replied, "We are, too," explaining patiently that each tribe had a different god.

One tribe worshiped the leopard. One night a leopard broke into the place where they were staying, causing much excitement among the Africans, who were quick to warn the missionaries that the leopard, as their god, would eat them when they died.

The missionaries showed the tribes people a copy of the Bible, pointing out the very first verse: "In the beginning God created the heavens and the earth," and "in the image of God he created them." The missionaries said, "Look, God created the leopard and in fact God created everything. God is not a leopard, God is God."

Now although each tribe had their own god and those gods could be very dangerous, there was one specific god all Africans knew about: the Creator of everything. But although the Africans believed in a creator God, they did not give him much attention because they believed the creator God had gone on a journey and would never come back again. In their minds, there were two kinds of gods: the tribal gods, who ruled mostly by fear and intimidation, and the god who had left.

The absent god.

There are at least six hundred stories across Africa about the creator God who goes away, never to return. One of my favorite stories comes from Ghana in West Africa, where God was nearby after he had created everything, and the women in the village were not happy because God was too close. So they whacked him in the face and in fury God went into the sky.

Well, this wasn't what they had wanted, so the women and the children collected mortars and stood one on top of the other while a woman climbed to the top of the tower to reach God. She was so close, but she needed one more barrel to reach God. When there were no more barrels a naughty little boy pulled a barrel from the bottom of the pile and the barrels came crashing down on the village.

The point of the story was clear.

God had left.

God would never return.

But when the missionaries came, they told the villages about Jesus, who is God with us and who came to Earth to save us. This news, in stark relief with their previous belief, explains their joy upon hearing the gospel. God has not, in fact, gone away, and he will never go away. He will never leave you nor forsake you.

Sunday by Sunday a few more villagers ventured to Katuru Hill, joining the missionaries sitting under the great tree. The creation of a new church had begun. I suppose there has been no Sunday over the last eighty years when there was no cluster of believers in Jesus worshiping on Katuru Hill.

Likewise for me there has never been a Sunday when I have not joined in worship with believers wherever I might be, except for when I have been ill or on the road, although I try to avoid traveling on Sundays. I suppose my parents even took me to the gathering at Shirati on the Sunday after I was born. I am now over eighty years old, and continue to revel in the joy of meeting and greeting the church gathered usually on Sundays. The Christian passion to gather as a church is a preparation for the day all God's people will gather and join in the heavenly choirs singing the joys of redemption. The core of the message that the missionaries brought was John 3:16: "For God so loved the world that he gave his one and only son, that whoever believes in him shall not perish but have eternal life."

Elam and Emil went to Musoma District headquarters to telegraph the good news that a welcoming place for the mission had been found. The name of the place was Shirati, about two miles from the lakeshore, and the missionaries were immediately met and welcomed by the chief. This served as further confirmation that they had chosen the right location,

The first Mennonite missionaries traveled from Mwanza to Shirati by a sailboat called a dhow similar to the one pictured here.

because from the beginning EMM had sought to enter a community where they were invited and welcomed.

The first team was comprised of Elam and Elizabeth Stauffer and John and Ruth Mosemann. The two couples arrived there to stay in 1934. They traveled along the lake's perimeter by dhow, a type of sailboat, and when they arrived at Shirati, they meandered up Katuru Hill alongside oxen, pitching their tents atop the hill about two miles from the lake. The local community assisted the two couples. Grass thatched roofs defended them from the rain. Imagine the couples cooking their first meals on Katuru Hill! Imagine those first days of life in that new place! How excited they must have felt to finally be there, among the people.

Within days of arrival on the hill, the missionaries had acquired nicknames. John Mosemann's name stuck. Masawa!

The great tree at Shirati, where the first missionaries pitched their tents. Hosted by Bishop John Nyagwegwe, 2012.

That means Hello—how are you? One usually uses that phrase for the first greeting of a new day, but John used Masawa repeatedly through the day, leading to the nickname. He added "Bwana" meaning "Mister." So he became Mister Hello. Soon the Katuru Hill also became Bwana Masawa. Today, all across Tanzania, Katuru Hill is known as Bwana Masawa, a legacy of those first missionary couples. It's a warm name suggesting an enthusiastic welcome.

Within some days of their arrival intense discussions developed about priorities. Some believed they should begin with the stories of Jesus, while others in the foursome team believed they should first develop a medical clinic. The argument for starting with Jesus' stories was that a clinic without a church would not have the spiritual foundations needed for authentic transformation, but on the other hand, presence with no medical ministry seemed quite heartless. This debate pushed this small team into serious missiological discernment.

They found a way. They would preach Jesus and they would emulate the healing ministry of Jesus: to this day at Shirati, the hospital and the church flow together. An obvious result of this decision is that in Shirati patients are invited for prayers and Scripture reading as well as receiving medical attention. The two have gone hand in hand since the beginning.

In this way they settled the conversation about whether to focus on medicine or evangelism, but that debate would never be far off. But wrestling with those questions around mission did lead them to three governing principles they would come to base their decisions on: would their actions lead to self-propagating, self-supporting, and self-governing churches? The little missionary team at Shirati were committed to planting those kinds of congregations.

Within a year another event of cultural and spiritual transformation occurred. John and Catherine Leatherman arrived to commence the Mennonite Bible school, beginning in Shirati. Five locals enrolled. After a year at Shirati, Leatherman, with those five new potential pastors, migrated to Nyabange, fifty miles south along the lake. That Bible school formed the theology of the Mennonites for many years to come. Years later when my brother was at the Bible College, he would arrange for me to come to Nyabange to do seminars in the Bible College.

It all seemed so right. Evangelism and medical ministry woven together in the seamless web of the gospel. And a Bible school!

Alas, dissonance occurred at the school, when John Leatherman exhibited a struggle with anger issues. Another missionary confessed that she lived with anger against the milk maid. There were also cultural issues which created dissonance: the missionary director tried to require the students to carry water

Comparing the Muslim and Christian understanding of scripture at the Mennonite Bible College located at Nyabangi, Tanzania, 2003.

one mile to the Bible school, but the students insisted that in African practice it is the women who carry the water. The Bible school had good theology but the praxis was strained.

Then one day, John received a surprising outpouring of the Holy Spirit after revival touched the church at Shirati and the emerging church in Nyabange. Significantly, after experiencing the Holy Spirit in such a profound way, John came to love his students, and he came to love Jesus in ways he had never anticipated, becoming a humble servant. When the community witnessed this new radiance of love in John's life, it challenged their own actions and ways of doing things. Mutual service in love and acting in humility became the community's goal.

Later, as a little boy growing up in that community, I knew I wanted to be like John some day because he was so kind and gracious. Seeing the practical ways that the Holy Spirit had changed this man created a desire in my heart to have the same transformational experience.

It was 1934 when my father Clyde asked his minister if he should go into missions. My parents left for Africa two years later, in 1936. They joined this already-established group of Mennonite missionaries, and my parents were based in the village hamlet of Bumangi eighteen miles from the lake, assigned to the Zanaki language people.

My childhood home was Bumangi.

For me personally, my journey began at the clinic in Shirati in Tanzania, where I was born in 1937.

My parents, Clyde and Alta Shenk, departing on the S.S. New York. They are dressed in the traditional garb of Mennonites in 1936.

2

Bumangi, Our Home

My first memory is of intense pain and a man examining my feet in the beam of a flashlight. I screamed—a kettle of boiling water had been accidentally spilled on my feet. I was probably around two years old at the time, and I still bear the scars these eighty years later. But my early childhood trauma was not nearly as terrible as the fate that awaited most Zanaki babies—infant mortality in Tanzania, when I was born, was 80 percent. I lived, while most Zanaki babies died.

EMM had given my parents the assignment of evangelizing a region where the gospel was not yet known. There were no schools and no literacy. Our first home was a tin shack, and because World War II was raging, there was no gasoline available for traveling. Mother bore all four of us there in the small hospital in Shirati (Joseph was born en route to the hospital and nearly died). She was well aware of the rate of infant mortality. Both of my parents put a lot on the line when they left the United States, but they were at peace about the potential sacrifices—to them, it was always about the call, and saying "Yes" to that call.

Tanganyika never felt like a sacrifice to me—it only felt like home. I grew up loving the wide meadows and long, sloping hills of Bumangi and the gracious, welcoming people. Some of my earliest memories are of my dad and mother taking me and Joseph down the hills to see some little waterfalls, and having a picnic lunch there. We sat by the falls, eating ugali with our fingers. Ugali was a very thick, darkish mush dipped in broth or greens. Tanzanians always ate with their fingers, and so did we.

My father holding me in front of my first home in Bumangi, Tanzania, in 1937.

I was troubled, though, at an early age, by the evidence I saw of a deep brokenness in the society. Too often I fell asleep hearing the cries of a wife being beaten in a nearby hamlet. Too often, I watched as women bore the brunt of the labor in the community.

In spite of all this, our mother often exclaimed, "My family, how blessed we are to serve and live among these wonderful people."

In those early days my parents dove into learning the Zanaki language along with Swahili, the trade language for Tanganyika. Mother picked up the language quickly as she visited hamlets, usually on her own or with one of us siblings, sharing stories of Jesus. The highest priority became translating the gospel of Matthew into Zanaki.

Dad and Metasela Nyagwaswa, a Christian man from a nearby tribe, began the translation process. Eugene Nida also joined us for several days—he was a linguist and an anthropology authority. I'll never forget him and his wife and the hilarious song they taught us:

The horses run around, their feet are on the ground.
Oh, who will wind the clock when I'm away?
Oh, a snake slips, because it has no hips,
but who built the shore so near the ocean?

After spending time with the Nidas, I became fascinated with their facility in language and the way they integrated culture and language.

Thanks to this small but solid team around my dad, the book of Matthew was finally translated and published—the first book ever published in Zanaki. Decades later, we would bring our children back to Bumangi, and during one of the church services we attended, with seven hundred people

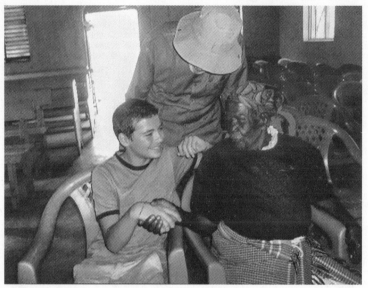

David and grandson Owen Corkery with Musse, who enjoys sharing her testimony—"The book of Matthew tells all about it," 2012.

present, one of the first believers in that community held a tattered booklet high and sang, "This book tells all about Jesus." Her name was Musse, and it was the gospel of Matthew that she held up above her head as she danced and sang her way through the congregation. I wept with joy. That was the book of Matthew, translated and published by my father and the team he had worked with.

Thirteen months after my arrival, my brother Joseph was born—we were a grand team from a young age, and it's a miracle that we survived our childhood, especially considering all of the escapades the two of us got into. As we grew older, Mother and Father were busy establishing this new community, particularly involved with setting up a school to teach reading and writing, so we brothers stirred up a fair amount of harmless (and occasionally harmful) mischief.

Due to our misbehaving, my brother Joseph and I decided that our father's life should be made a little easier, so we cut the branches off a small tree in the yard for him to use as switches anytime one of us needed to be disciplined. Father wasn't impressed—we had practically ruined one of the trees he had so carefully planted and nurtured.

Even when our motives were innocent, Joseph and I managed to get into trouble. Especially grievous to me was the day I took Dad's trumpet out of its case, dropped it, and ruined the lovely horn, a disobedience that took from my Dad one of his most loved hobbies, playing the trumpet. He still played occasionally, but that beautiful instrument was crinkled and quite ugly after that.

Still, our regular readings of Scripture were a balm to my soul, giving me a sense of tranquility and security, and it was at that early age that I learned to find peace in Jesus.

Another incident involved my parents' car, which was jacked up and useless due to a lack of available fuel during World War II. On an ordinary afternoon, in an act of boredom and carelessness, one of our boyhood playmates accidentally set the house and car alight. The fire damaged the house and completely gutted the car, although without fuel it had been useless anyway. As a boy, I wasn't aware of the particulars of how this loss might have affected my parents, but now I wonder. Did it feel like a major blow to them, or did the automobile's uselessness in time of a fuel shortage truly mean it was an ancillary loss? I now know, after many years living abroad, how I've written off some losses rather easily while deeply mourning others.

Around that time Dad realized he could use kerosene for his little Wanderer cycle—with gas to start the engine, and kerosene to power it, we could travel without gasoline. Occasionally, Dad invited one of the children to go with him on the motorcycle as he made his weekend preaching circuits. Which was nice, because for a period of time we came to dread Sundays at our own church, a grass-roofed building with an earth floor . . . infested with jiggers. We didn't wear shoes, so the access into our toenails was like a conduit for those bugs. The removal of jiggers became an essential dimension of church attendance. When Dad found an antidote for jiggers—iodine—that was a happy day.

But one thing we loved about Sunday was the games Mother organized for the children in our community. And as we became closer friends with our neighbors, they took us on

Enjoying the pushcart Dad made, with Joseph watching, c. 1939.

hunting trips and lakeshore fishing at Nyabange. One morning I was playing outside with my African friends and I ran into the house, calling to my mother, "I am a very happy little boy!" Then I continued on with my play. Those were wonderful days. I can think of no better place to be a child than Bumangi in the 1940s.

When I was still small, my father, along with an associate, cut down a tree for a house they were building, but the men didn't know that they had taken the tree from a sacred grove, considered by the Zanaki to be the location of their community's gods and spirits. The elders of the clan prepared for conflict, alarmed at what they must have seen as destructive and offensive behavior by these newcomers.

This was one of my parents' first great conundrums—to cease and desist cutting trees down from that grove would be a signal that Christians venerated the trees and agreed that the grove was holy. To continue felling trees from that grove would communicate that we did not believe there were divine spirits in the grove, that we didn't believe in their gods, yet that was an act that could raise serious opposition, perhaps even violence.

Some of the townspeople dug graves for our family, an awful premonition. That day, a dozen women with their witches' paraphernalia danced around our home. They had welcomed the missionaries when they arrived, but this intrusion into what they considered sacred ground aroused their divinities and spirits. The powers of death and life collided around that shrine.

One of the men from the Zanaki tribe who had become a Christian said that if we proceeded, the possibility of death was real; however, if we stopped, they would say the power of the gods was real and had interrupted our work. This man and his wife were the only African Christians in our community at the time. It was a lonely struggle for our small group, deciding best how to confront the people and their belief in these tribal gods.

"As for me," the solitary African believer said. "I think we should keep working and treat the grove like any other grove of trees. We have nothing to fear. Jesus is Lord."

My father continued on with the project, taking only what was needed, and we did not die. Somehow, conflict was averted, and my parents and the other missionaries were allowed to continue on with their work. Perhaps the local people believed that if the gods wanted to intervene, they would have done so.

And yet in my heart, I wonder. Even to this day, I don't know if my father should have cut down the trees in that grove. They didn't have the benefit of hindsight or of a manual telling them what to do in certain situations. Could there have been an alternative way forward, one that included an explanation on how we viewed trees while not disturbing the site?

Yet, maybe my father and the other missionaries did the right thing in forging ahead and using trees from that sacred grove. We had experienced an important moment in confrontation with demonic powers. Years later, one of the women engaged in that confrontation came to church on a Sunday morning to burn all her witchcraft items, declaring that she knew Jesus was Lord and she would no longer practice witchcraft.

God was working, and revival was coming, though no one could see it at the time.

As the conflict between the dozen believers and tribal elders intensified, my father had concerns for our well-being. Our neighbor who was an expert in the occult had peered into my parents' bedroom in the heart of the night, striking terror into our father. Often Dad sang his favorite hymn, "Jesus is a Wall of Fire Around Us," and even as a young boy I could tell that he sang it with more gusto when he was feeling especially concerned.

We were surrounded by conflict, and soon these struggles came into our own home when the father of a twelve-year-old girl named Wakuru had arranged for her marriage to an elderly polygamous man. Several girls, along with Wakuru, were learning about following Jesus, but Wakuru's parents said she couldn't attend the classes anymore. Still, Wakuru continued coming to the Bible study, and as she learned more about Jesus, she determined that if Jesus loved her, then he would not foist this marriage on her. She firmly refused.

The Zanaki tribe was pulled into the struggle. Never before had a young girl been empowered to resist a marriage arranged by her father. In fact, cows for the dowry had already been exchanged, making the marriage, in the eyes of the tribe, indissoluble. Wakuru, still refusing the marriage, was beaten and chained. When alone in her hut, she sang quietly a song she had learned in her Bible classes: "There's Not a Friend Like the Lowly Jesus."

> There's not a friend like the lowly Jesus:
> No, not one! No, not one!
> None else could heal all our soul's diseases:
> No, not one! No, not one!
>
> Jesus knows all about our struggles;
> He will guide till the day is done:
> There's not a friend like the lowly Jesus:
> No, not one! No, not one!

The struggle went on for over a year. On one occasion three of Wakuru's brothers appeared in our church during a worship service, shouting, "Wakuru, come with us!" as they charged into the auditorium. They grabbed her, but my father went directly to the back entrance, blocking them from taking her. He then escorted the three men to the outside and sat with them on the ground in a circle, imploring them to respect Wakuru's freedom to follow Christ. Wakuru collected and returned their clubs, a sign of forgiveness for previous beatings, and then went on her way.

Some time later there was another attack—this time at our home. At least a dozen people encircled the house, threw rocks, and verbally threatened us, all while my dad was not at home. I was five years old at that time, and Mother asked me to hold the door shut as she looked for the key in order to lock it. Wakuru had quickly entered our house and vanished from sight, causing her family to target us. Eventually, when we refused to open the door or hand her over, the people left, and my brother and I shifted our boxes in the attic, trying to find her hiding place. Finally, we discovered her under my bed, shaking like a leaf, tight against the wall. Mother took her, embraced her, and encouraged her.

The conflict we experienced in those early days wasn't just between us and the tribespeople—often the society itself was divided between two of its own clans, the Blacksmiths and the Basket Makers. They prohibited marrying across those clans, so when Wakuru and Meso Nyakitumu became engaged, one a Blacksmith, the other a Basket Maker, the Zanaki people were very concerned. After months of negotiations it became clear that the tribal elders would not agree for a Basket Maker and Blacksmith to marry, so Wakuru and Meso had the first Christian wedding within the Zanaki region without the blessing of family or tribe. Their tribe cursed them to childlessness.

Nevertheless, God blessed them with thirteen children! Sadly, the youngest was stricken with cerebral malaria. Her parents did not abandon her and instead loved and cared for their invalid daughter. Tribal elders believed the malaria was lingering punishment for not submitting to the ways of the ancestors; nevertheless, the care of those parents for their daughter was a powerful witness of the love of God ministering even to those who are disadvantaged.

Wakuru's husband Meso was my father's dear friend. When they first met, Meso was a student at the school, and he showed up two hours early because he didn't want to be late. My father invested forty years in mission in Tanzania and Kenya, and eventually Wakuru and Meso became the pastor couple at Bumangi, the very church where I grew up. So these two families, the Shenks and the Nyakitumus, continued their friendships for many years after the churches in the Bumangi area were well established. When my father died, I kept in touch with the Nyakitumu family, who have meant so much to our family over the years.

One day not too long ago, many decades after I had left Tanzania, a large envelope arrived with the carefully written description of the fiftieth wedding anniversary of Meso and Wakuru. He described how some five hundred people came for the celebration. A bull was slaughtered. The honored couple were given new clothing. Choirs sang songs written for the event. Children and grandchildren were there. Bishops and pastors as well as government and tribal authorities were present. The whole congregation walked the mile from the Nyakitumu home, all the way to the church.

In polygamous homes there is never any celebration of a wedding anniversary. The emergence of monogamous marriage is one of the treasured gifts of the gospel. The whole of Zanaki society was a participant in this anniversary celebration, at least vicariously, and joy permeated the event. And it

Meso and Wakuru celebrating our visit to Bumangi with a goat feast.

Bumangi choir who sang to celebrate a visit by David and Grace and sister
Anna Kathryn.

had all began in the soul of twelve-year-old Wakuru, who had refused the marriage arranged by her father and said of Meso, "Because of Jesus I will marry the man I love."

The wedding anniversary was a high-profile event, but often change happens more unobtrusively. Meso told us of an experience shortly after he and Wakuru were married. The two of them often walked a couple of miles to the public market. While returning, Wakuru asked Meso to carry the groceries because she had a headache, but Meso refused because carrying groceries was a woman's responsibility, not the responsibility of the husband. It would be humiliating for him to do so.

Down the road Meso discovered that Wakuru wasn't carrying the groceries anymore. He asked where the groceries were. She said, "I told you that I have a headache. It is your money that bought the groceries. They are yours."

Meso apologized for not listening to her need for help. He returned up the road and carried the groceries home, an action unheard of in Zanaki society – a husband carrying groceries for his wife! Imagine the mirth in the market that day when Meso, the Christian, carried the groceries home. On one occasion she told me, "Meso never beat me even once. But he did love me and kindly encouraged me."

Indeed, the presence of a small church within Zanaki society had brought transformations, large and small.

I still have wonderful memories of our evenings there in Bumangi.

When night fell, my job was to light the kerosene lanterns, and we gathered around to hear Mother read Bible stories and other stories to us over and over again. She was a good teacher of theology. I have treasured Mother's stories and have carried with me a commitment to telling stories to children in homes and churches where we meet. Storytelling to the children is a great joy. When we were on vacation, sometimes Dad would tell us family stories or other stories from the Bible that he loved, and it was through this family time together, hearing Scripture, that I knew Jesus was central to our lives and everything that our family was engaged in. My parents' love for the Word of God formed me.

In time, our father's love for the Word led him into memorizing Scripture. He committed to memory both the books of Ephesians and Hebrews, and when invited to do so, he would proclaim these memorized books with power. Later, he offered a free bicycle to any church leader who recited Hebrews by memory.

Sometimes, as mother traveled from hamlet to hamlet, she got lost in the rolling Bumangi hills, but there were no phones for her to call our father to come and fetch her. If Mother wasn't home by a certain time, Dad would ring the church bell, helping mother regain her orientation. Often, when the bell sounded, local children would find her and help her on her way. She loved those children so much, and one of her first loves was teaching these people who had never seen a Bible or heard of Jesus. Since she couldn't speak the language, she often used pictures to tell the stories.

It's a beautiful image to me even today—the children of Bumangi, racing to help my mother find her way, gathering around her and bringing her home. How many of those children did she help lead to their spiritual home?

3

Fire on Katuru Hill

When I was seven years old, I remember the thunderstorm that brought down destruction on our community. The pulpit of the grass thatched church was hit by a bolt of lightning. Dad went to his bedroom and threw himself before the Lord, imploring God to send torrents of rain to extinguish the fire. No rain came, and the church burned to the ground.

Undaunted, the small congregation at Bumangi rebuilt the church. I enjoyed rebuilding the church. We gathered grass for the roof and loaded it on the pick-up truck. I sat on top of the huge mound of grass with my brother Joseph. There were chameleons on the trees above and I delighted in watching them change colors.

The fire that happened that day was a physical fire that caused much damage. But there was another fire coming, the fire of the Holy Spirit's convicting power, a fire that would change all of us.

The first Bumangi church building. The roof was rebuilt after a lightning bolt hit it.

When I look back on all that happened in those early days, I am in awe. After all, my parents were among the first missionaries to this part of the world. There was no handbook. Everything that came at them was new, and they had to make the best decisions they could in the moment. Their dedication to the community, along with their willingness to say "Yes" to Jesus, carried them a long way.

But despite the fervor of the missionaries and all the progress that had been made, not all was well within the churches. Few Africans were seeking baptism—only three had become members at Nyabange, the Mennonite mission center, and this was after ten years of prayer and missions work. Discouragement ran so deeply that members of the missionary team considered returning to America, and some of the African church leaders asked EMM to remove the missionaries and appoint better ones.

You can imagine the effect this had on my parents and their friends.

Orie Miller, who was visiting at the time, stood up and began to cry, insisting that the charges weren't true. His tears came with a bold proclamation that we needed to trust and respect each other, despite what first appeared to be disappointing results.

I remember as a teenager seeing a tiny white paper in my father's office window, and on it he had written the words, "Don't pity yourself." When I asked him about it, he said he thought the African people would cherish the gospel—after all, that's why he had left home and gone all the way to East Africa to be a missionary! But he quickly discovered that most Africans had no interest in the gospel. Ten years had passed in Bumangi, with little response.

But I must give you another image, one from fifty years in the future, when I visited Bumangi on a Sunday morning. The church was packed with seven hundred people sharing their testimonies. Dad wept and leaned toward me, whispering, "Son, I would do it again! This is so wonderful."

At the height of this discouragement, Elam Stauffer called on the church leadership to join in several days of prayer— he traveled one hundred miles on his own from Shirati to Mwanza to meet with Emil Sywalka and several others for prayer and council. An assembly gathered at Shirati, yearning for the healing grace of the Holy Spirit. Together, they waited for Elam to return.

When he did, the congregation continued to gather, but in silence. This was August 9, 1943.

Then it happened.

The fire of the Holy Spirit's convicting power fell upon the assembly with a profound conviction of sin, and those assembled burst into tears of repentance. It sounded like the fire of God described in Acts 2:18b-19a.

I will pour out my spirit in those days, and they will proph-
esy. I will show wonders in the heavens above and signs on
the earth below.

Soon, joy permeated the assembly—there were large boulders adjacent to our home, and one evening the youth sang all
night, sitting on those boulders, celebrating their joy in Christ.

Years later, I was sitting with Bishop Kisare by the great
tree where the first Mennonite missionaries had embarked by
dhow seventy years before. I asked the dear bishop brother
about the revival. "What happened here at Katuru Hill those
many years ago?"

Tears trickled down his cheeks as he responded, "You are
referring to the day the fire of God fell on Katuru Hill. That

Bishop Zedekia Kisare, first African bishop, sharing with me under the tree. "No
thought has ever entered my mind more amazing than this: Jesus Christ, God's
son, died for my sins and I am forgiven," c. 1997.

day God touched me and began his transforming work in my soul. My calling as a minister of the gospel began that day. That was a day I shall never forget. Jesus touched me and transformed me. People bypassed Katuru Hill, for the word in the villages was that all who come near will be burned for the fire of God is burning on Katuru Hill."

The word began to spread among the nonbelievers in the area: stay away from the revival. The fire of God had fallen on Katuru Hill, and anyone who went near would be burned. They recognized the need for conversion, the need for their sins to be taken away, but many of them were afraid of this new fire. The revivalists were nicknamed *balokole*, or "the people on fire for Christ."

What happened those several days in Shirati was happening all across East Africa. There is a mystery in the ministry of the Holy Spirit. Jesus said we hear and see the fruit of the Holy Spirit, but we know not from where the Spirit comes. So it was within the East Africa Revival Fellowship. John 3:8, "The wind blows wherever it pleases. You hear its sound, but you cannot tell where it comes from or where it is going. So it is with everyone born of the Spirit."

Our home was touched with joy and peace, and the revival was touching people outside our home as well. For example, an elderly man had married a Christian, and he would beat her when she attended church. The counsel of the church was for her to submit to her husband and cease attending church for the present. Such respect led her husband to seek Jesus, and he was converted. The husband then walked twenty-four miles to meet the church leaders to ask them and his wife for forgiveness for the ways he had mistreated her. I would be deeply impressed by the East Africa Revival Fellowship for many years to come.

On that August Sunday when the congregation experienced the convicting fire of God, people wept in repentance throughout the day and into the evening hours. Two twelve-year-old students at the Shirati elementary school, Wilson Ogwada Okach and Nikanor Dhaje, experienced such compassion for the lost that they left school for some time to go from village to village preaching the gospel. They became the first African Mennonite missionaries as they traveled from community to community to proclaim the word of God. They pressed onward along the Kenya-Tanzania borderlands even though they were beaten at least once.

In the providence of God, Rebecca Kinziza Okendo (known as "Speedy") opened her home on the Kenya border for the Tanzanian emissaries of the gospel. Speedy got her name because she walked so fast, traveling twenty-four kilometers on foot each day. Through her speed-walking she knit together a relationship between the Kenyan revivalists and the Tanzanian revivalists. Her legacy endures in the form of fellowships of believers along the Kenya-Tanzania Lake Victoria borderlands.

Early on, the revivalists discerned the need for ways that sustain the ministry of the Holy Spirit for the East Africa Fellowship. This meant meeting regularly for fellowship, confession, and repentance.

And the Holy Spirit also touched me.

A group of missionaries met at Mugango for their annual conference, and a missionary explained to the children that Jesus is our Savior. There was something beautiful about the stories she told. Her voice rang in my heart and mind, and that evening I couldn't go to sleep. Quietly, I got out of bed, walked through the dark house, and knocked on my parents' door.

"I need Jesus," I whispered, kneeling with my parents and confessing that I was a sinner who needed Jesus to be my Savior. I felt a baptism of joy sweep over me, and even after returning to my bed, I couldn't fall asleep for that overwhelming joy. Early that morning, before anyone else woke up, I slipped into a nearby chapel and sat by the second window on the left. That morning, alone, I covenanted with Jesus to follow him all the days of my life.

I had a clear sense that Jesus was calling me to be a missionary among those who did not know him, and that calling solidified my joy and gave me an immense amount of certainty and comfort about the direction of my life. That call, and my "Yes" to that calling, has been the most important event of my life. From that day until today I have not doubted that Jesus is my Savior, and that I am called to be an emissary of Jesus, especially among unreached people. The calling has been that simple and that clear, and I am forever grateful. As a boy, I never could have seen the long, meandering path that call would lead me on.

It was around that time that my brother, Joseph, and I noticed our Father beginning every morning with a time of Bible reading and prayer. So, after that evening when Christ called me, we asked our father to have devotions with us before our day began.

One morning during this devotional time, Father read the passage in John 15:1-5 (KJV), describing the vine and the branches:

I am the true vine, and my Father is the husbandman.

Every branch in me that beareth not fruit he taketh away: and every branch that beareth fruit, he purgeth it, that it may bring forth more fruit.

Now ye are clean through the word which I have spoken
unto you.

Abide in me, and I in you. As the branch cannot bear fruit
of itself, except it abide in the vine; no more can ye, except
ye abide in me.

I am the vine, ye are the branches: He that abideth in me,
and I in him, the same bringeth forth much fruit: for without me ye can do nothing.

A storm had recently torn a branch from the trunk of
a tree, and our father pointed out the tree to Joseph and
me. The place where the branch had been wrenched from
the tree was broken and splintered. Our father observed
that the branch severed from the trunk would die—it could
not live on its own. I felt an incredible emptiness, looking at
that broken branch.

Father said something that day I've never forgotten: "Jesus
is our eternal trunk."

That devotional has largely formed my approach in daily
repentance and spirituality all my life. I determined to have
time with Jesus and the Word before beginning my day. It was
Orie Miller, that early visitor to the African continent, exploring the best place for Mennonite missionaries to settle, who
encouraged the international teams he led to carry the Bible in
the right hand and Time magazine in the left. In essence, I have
always done that, as the Word and the current context have
significantly formed my spiritual discipline.

In this way, the revival that came from the fire that fell
on Katuru Hill continued. My father's passion for the gospel
wasn't limited to personal devotions, and it didn't wane as
the weeks passed. He took every opportunity he had to share
it with the people. One day, he got permission from the British

officers, then took a paintbrush out to major rock formations throughout the Musoma district and painted Scripture verses on them with references. Most of the verses he chose were from the gospel of John, including his favorite, John 3:16.

"For God so loved the world, that he gave his only begotten Son, that whosoever believeth in him should not perish, but have everlasting life" (KJV).

As time went on, and the British were not in charge anymore, a customs officer found out that Dad was the one who had painted these large verses on the rocks.

"Sir," the man asked. "Are you the one painting words on the rocks?"

"Yes," my dad replied. "Those are verses from the holy Scriptures."

"You need to wash that writing off of the rocks," the man said.

Dad pulled out the papers showing the permission he had received from the British government while they were in charge. "I've received permission. It's okay."

"No, it's not," the man insisted. "That was another administration. I will not tolerate this—you need to go out and wash these words off of the rocks."

"Sir," my Dad said again. "I received permission to do it. I can't bring myself to erase Scripture, those words that mean so much to me. If they have to be taken off, you may decide what to do, but I can't do it. I just can't."

The officer thought about it for a moment, then relented.

"Okay, I accept that. But don't do it again."

For years after that, on eight or so large rocks along the road, Scripture verses bore witness to the gospel.

My dad's actions inspired me to share the word of God enthusiastically.

In fact, my dad's life inspired me to make sacrifices of my own. I had been saving money to buy my own bicycle, doing odd jobs around the house and the neighborhood. It was at this time that our congregation at Bumangi prepared to send out our first missionary couple to a neighboring clan, and when I heard they would be taking an offering for the couple, I knew in my heart I needed to give what I could. I took the money I was saving for a bike and gave half of it in the offering to support this couple, sending out our first missionary. I can still remember the sermon at that missionary-sending event, and the Scripture it was based on: Matthew 24:14.

"And this gospel of the kingdom will be preached in the whole world as a testimony to all nations, and then the end will come."

Even at an early age, I was learning what it was like to live in a mission-minded way.

When it came time for the mission to build, the chief of the Zanaki clan, among whom we lived, allotted a gently sloping hill for our home. The chief was the sole distributor of parcels of land, and I'm sure my parents were encouraged that they would have a plot of land to develop. On the slope were several white anthills, huge mounds full of insects that would destroy any structure. My father realized that our hill was a litmus test—if the ants destroyed the building, then all would know that the mission was not good for the Zanaki people. On the other hand, if the missionaries destroyed the anthills so that the schools and development programs flourished, then everyone would recognize that the mission was good for the Zanaki of Bumangi.

The trick was to kill the mother ant, much like destroying a queen bee in a beehive. As a child, I was intrigued when the workmen began digging down into the anthill. One foot, two feet down, and there they found the fat, one-inch long mother ant. Once the mother ant was removed, the ant hills slowly degenerated into dust.

As I watched, a pastor explained to me that within the Zanaki culture were evils that needed to be destroyed, just as the workmen were digging in to destroy the mother ant. The anthill was a metaphor of sin within culture—only Jesus could go to the root of evil and transform a community.

Providentially, the anthills died off and the first school among the Zanaki flourished. Superstition was giving way. And while the church brought about a spiritual revival, the missionaries' focus on education brought about its own sort of renewal within the culture.

Education was a great gift my parents brought to the Zanaki people. There was such a passion for literacy throughout the area; unbeknownst to my parents, they had arrived on the cusp of an enormous push for education. The British colonial government had come together with the emerging Tanganyika government to push for two things: freedom and education.

Imagine this: in 1936, as far as my parents could tell, no one was literate within the Zanaki tribe where my parents were serving. By the end of that decade, the push for literacy began, and Bumangi was chosen as the place where post-primary education would develop within the region.

This is not to say that interest in education was universal—some communities in Musoma District resisted schools, but chiefs, encouraging their people to send their children, sometimes offered a goat to any father whose child attended school. Men and boys in the tribes were often surprised by how quickly the girls learned. Some Muslim communities were hesitant, but as time passed, more and more parents embraced the idea of their children receiving an education.

Some missionaries voiced concern that educational growth would become a greater priority than evangelistic ministry. Would emerging commitments to schools and hospitals weaken the church? Some were disturbed that after ten years of mission in five locations there were only 313 members in the Tanganyika church—would all of this focus on education keep the newly planted churches from thriving?

These questions have, incredibly enough, persisted in the Mennonite mission field for nearly a century! Missionaries still find it difficult to unite on what it looks like to balance evangelism and philanthropy. Nevertheless, medical and educational development emerged in Tanganyika alongside the blossoming political systems that would encourage modern statehood.

I still remember waking in the middle of the night to the sound of drums and choirs singing—the singers had marched for days to Bumangi where they would help build the first middle school.

Youth work crews arrived from each of the five Mennonite mission centers, and my job was to help my father with the measuring strings for the walls and foundations. It was generally a picture of mass chaos! Yet the whole experience of joy was beyond imagination. Tribal groups came together to work on the project, tribes who had never cooperated before. It was a miracle.

A school was born that imprinted upon the future in unforgettable ways, shaping society. Within a decade, Mennonite primary schools enrolled over four thousand students, and the high school held six hundred. By the early 1950s, the majority in the area could read and write. The leap from a preliterate society to one that embraced modern education was utterly phenomenal.

My parents, teaching the ABCs, had no clue about the true significance of what they were doing: profoundly changing a culture through education.

The great European wars ceased, and churches in Bumangi grew. Many young men and women back in the United States who might have considered a missions vocation had died in the wars. The loss of so much life was mourned around the world after World War II ended. Still, village life for us continued on.

I was enjoying being eight years old—we finally had a working vehicle, a pickup truck, and on one particular day all of us were driving to the Bible school building when we saw Elam Stauffer approaching, looking very serious. We pulled to the side of the dirt road and stopped.

Elam spoke through the driver's side window of our pickup. "Ray Wenger died last night."

How could it be true? Ray and his wife had a fruitful ministry, and he was the father of three of our playmates; one of their sons was my age. He had died from complications of malaria—my father always assumed death might come his way, and if it did, it would most likely be brought by mosquitoes. Even I grew up knowing I was quite prone to malaria, and that following Jesus might mean laying down one's life.

But on that morning, June 9, 1945, it was Ray Wenger who was called by Jesus. We turned around and drove the twenty-four miles to Mugango and the Wenger home. Their grief was deep. The funeral took place that afternoon.

I found a quiet place alone, and I cried. I never imagined that Ray Wenger's widow would someday become stepmother to us Shenk siblings.

A few years later our family learned that the missionary agency had approved a one-year home leave. My parents had been in Bumangi for over a decade and would now have the opportunity to see their families. However, the departure port of Mombasa, newly opened since the end of the war, was overwhelmed by expatriates seeking ways to get home.

The message from the travel agencies was for all Europeans and Americans to remain in their homes until their transport was available. Those were exciting days as we packed our things and prepared to travel the six hundred miles from Nyabange to Mombasa, Kenya's port city.

And from there?

Back to the United States, a place I had never been.

4

Science as a Gift from God

We were waiting for word to arrive that we could begin our long journey to America. News first arrived via the grapevine: a woman at afternoon prayers said the Lord told her the time for the Shenks to leave is at hand. Then, a letter arrived from my grandparents in the United States: the Lord is saying the Shenks should leave now. My parents soon felt the same leading in their personal prayers, so we gathered our bags and traveled six hundred miles to the coast. We traveled by lake steamer to Kisumu, a lake port in Kenya, then by train to Nairobi where we spent the night, and finally by train through the night to Mombasa. When we arrived in Mombasa, we learned that the remaining Americans had left for the United States that morning, and we would be at the head of the line for the next steamer.

Six weeks later, we boarded the James Harlan, on our way.

Miriam Wenger, whose husband Ray had died so recently, joined us, along with her three children. There were only two cabins on this freighter, and we stopped at every port on the northeast side of the African continent. It was a fifty-four-day trip, and between Cape Town and Trinidad we saw no land for three weeks. Our freighter leaked steam, sometimes meandering in the ocean at the snail's pace of four mph. It was on that long trip when I learned my multiplication tables.

It was early March when we hit the ocean, and a tremendous cold front moved in. It was terrible—Father was certain we would slide right off the icy deck.

"You're experiencing a real American winter," Father warned us, teeth chattering.

Grasping the rails, Dad carefully climbed into the captain's command center.

"How cold is it?" he asked the captain.

"Fifty-four degrees!" the pilot said.

Arriving in Boston, we met our grandparents and cousins for the first time. We wept. Crew members wept. It was wonderful. After meeting our families in the Boston harbor, we drove through the night to Lancaster, jabbering the whole way. We were shocked that most of the trees in America were dead, or at least appeared so. In Africa, trees thrived. We were astonished to see such devastation. We were astonished by the streetlights. We were shocked when a policeman stopped our car for going too fast.

We stayed for a week with my mother's family and then for the duration of our furlough in the home of my father's family. I remember waking up, the air cold, hearing a bell ringing—Grandmother informed us that this was a telephone. I was completely astounded. For the next week or so, whenever the phone rang, all four of us raced down the stairs to grab it. None of us had ever seen such amazing technology.

What an amazing year it was in the States. My brother Joseph and I had ample opportunity at school and church to tell our peers about the wonders of Africa and the joys of hunting. The school even orchestrated a funding campaign, raising money for a bicycle for me and my brother to be purchased upon our return back in East Africa.

We stayed with relatives while our parents went off to a Summer Training Institute in Oklahoma for translators. Meanwhile, the farms of our respective grandparents were in full harvest—peach harvest was at hand, and the local paper sent out a reporter to see these "Africans" (my siblings and me) enjoying their first peaches.

A cousin who knew a pilot arranged for my brother and me to fly to Washington. I thought it was fun being a celebrity, and the Washington Post even planned on running a feature, but when Dad returned home late that night, he was not amused, calling the press and insisting the feature not be run. That would have been too much visibility for these gentle Mennonites.

It was a grand summer.

And then it was over.

Our year in the States passed by much too fast. I was eleven years old. It was 1948. In March, we began the long journey back to East Africa aboard the Marine Carp, a troopship and our ride back to the African continent. While most passengers were placed in large curtained halls with bunks that lined the gunwale sides of the ship, our family had a cabin. We set sail for Italy, then Haifa. Our ship stopped in Genoa, and Jews only recently released from concentration camps and refugee camps were attempting to find passage from their destroyed European homes to Israel.

On the first leg of our journey my father and a Jewish man became friends. The Jewish man's name was Jonas, the same name as my father's. They had Bible studies together on the ship. Father demonstrated through the Scriptures that when Israel returns to Palestine, that will be the destiny of all history, for that would be the fulfilment of prophecy. My father yearned that his friend Jonas would believe Jesus is the promised Messiah. Tears sometimes wet the cheeks of these two men named Jonas, the one proclaiming that Jesus is the promised Messiah, the other that the Messiah is sure to come soon and establish the reign of God on earth. For both men the coming of the Messiah was necessary for the kingdom of God to become present in its fullness. Both believed that promise was being fulfilled in the significant number of Jews returning to Israel. I don't know that they ever saw each other again after that voyage.

We stopped at Haifa, and all night, depth charges exploded in the harbor, deterring refugees from jumping overboard and swimming to shore. During the day, gun boats patrolled the water, ready to intercept anyone who tried to make their way from the ship to land. The atmosphere on the ship was tense as we waited to disembark. Finally, we moved on to Alexandria. I have no idea what happened to the hundreds of Jews who tried so desperately to get ashore at the various ports where we stopped—the raw traumas resulting from the Holocaust touched everyone. So many people were looking for new places to call home. It wasn't long after our journey that the Israeli-Palestinian war exploded, leading to the establishment of the state of Israel.

From that troopship, we found a train from Alexandria to Cairo. We needed to get to Kisumu as soon as possible. After all, there were six of us, room and board were not inexpensive, and as the weeks passed, our travel agent devoured more of our money. Our parents considered taking the Nile River through the desert. Fortunately, just as we spent the last of our money, bookings became available on Air France. I remember wondering if our travel agent had deliberately held up our reservations until we ran out of cash.

I loved the flight to Kisumu, the Sahara Desert stretching long and empty beneath us. Upon arrival, Joseph and I were bundled off to the train for the overnight ride to Kijabe, Kenya, where we were bivouacked for a semester with a hundred other missionary children.

One of the parents rode by train with the children and youth to the Rift Valley Academy (RVA), a boarding school we had been enrolled in. These plans were all new to me—I suppose everything was decided among the various missionary parents traveling together on the Marine Carp.

Joseph and I did not enjoy RVA. There were some older fellows who bullied us, one of whom rammed a pipe in my mouth, leaving me in terrible pain. Kijabe is rainy and muddy, and our clothing was rarely cleansed of the mud streaks. But we weren't the only ones—most of the children struggled to get the streaks of red mud out of their pants and shirts. Joseph and I prayed every day that Jesus would return, bringing to an end our experience in this school. Because of this, we developed a keen interest in theologies of the second coming of Jesus.

Then, an answer to prayer: all Mennonites would transfer to the Mennonite school developing in Nyabange in Tanganyika. Mother had homeschooled me for grades one and two, until the mission developed a school for missionary children, and this was the boarding school that we returned to and attended during the week. Then, the blessed weekend would arrive.

Every Saturday morning at school, someone would ring the bell and all of us Shenk siblings would run up the hill to catch the truck for the one-hour ride on top of the oil drums to our home in Bumangi. The truck ferried barrels of oil to a German-operated gold mine, and we loved riding on top of those barrels. That's how we made the eighteen-mile trek home.

We enjoyed Saturday night and Sunday at home—by Monday, the truck picked us up again and deposited us at Nyabange, the central mission station where the boarding school was developing.

One thing that changed our lives as missionary kids was the day we received a bicycle as a gift from our friends at the Willow Street, Pennsylvania, school for Joseph and me to share. We loved that bike. Sometimes, we sat along the road and called out John 3:16 to passing trucks. Those were happy

Enjoying the bicycle in Tanzania contributed by schoolmates at Willow Street School in Pennsylvania, 1948.

Growing up at Bumangi, left to right: Daniel, John, Anna Kathryn, Joseph, and David, c. 1950.

years for us Shenk children, all five of us by then, four boys and a girl: me, Joseph, Anna Kathryn, John, and Daniel. Bumangi had so many options for play and hunting, and as more and more families joined the ranks of Christians, our circle of friends increased.

One Saturday morning when we were waiting to return home for the weekend from our boarding school, the truck arrived earlier than usual to take us back to our home. The word for truck in British English is *lorry*, and someone came running down the hill to the school to let us know the truck was early—they shouted all the way down the hill, "The lorry is coming! The lorry is coming!"

Our teacher ran from the school and, looking into the sky, shouted, "Praise the Lord!" She had thought the voice shouting, "The lorry is coming," was actually saying, "The Lord is coming," and she thought the second coming of Christ was at hand.

Another precious day came when I was 12 years old, and I was baptized at the church in Shirati along with my brother and one other missionary child. I will always remember the joy of that day, as a congregation four hundred strong sang "O Happy Day."

Oh, happy day, indeed.

In hindsight it is easy for me to see how the missionary children's school was a minor element compared with the other developments taking place among the Zanaki people at the time. During the nearly ten years our family was developing the first Zanaki church, another astounding transformation was let loose among the Zanaki people—while our family was enjoying America for the first time, a tremendous revolution came to Bumangi, and then all of Africa, by way of the peoples who live among the Congo River forests. They discerned that people who chewed the bark from the quinine tree did not get malaria.

I was eleven when we returned to East Africa after a one-year home leave, and while Joseph and I were in boarding school and then making the transition to the missionary school, Mother, along with her associate, resumed their medical ministry on the front stoop of our home. The killer of the babies in the village was mostly malaria, so they began giving the babies quinine to get them through it—it was a preventer, but everyone in the village believed the true cause was witchcraft. Grandparents were sometimes suspected of being witches and were abandoned, often along with the infected children.

One day, a porter brought mother a wooden box—it came from Nairobi, five hundred miles away. They opened the box, and Mother's assistant placed a drop of blood on a glass slide in front of the microscope. One by one, everyone looked through the eyepieces and caught their first glimpse of a parasite. I was there on that momentous day.

"The cause of malaria is this parasite," the man said. "We will kill the parasite. We will pray that through medical science, the parasites killing your babies and grandparents will be eradicated."

Two days later, we returned to the one-room clinic and took a look in the microscope. The parasites were dead. The babies lived. Even the grandparents were given a reprieve in their old age, no longer blamed for the disease. It was the parasites, not bewitched grandparents, that brought death.

It is impossible to exaggerate the significance of what happened that day at the clinic in Bumangi. Science had taken a huge step forward in the fight against witchcraft and the fight against malaria. Nearby tribes even gave my parents a nickname that meant, "saviors of our tribe," a recognition that the scientific revolution brought into the Zanaki society had saved lives.

The healing of the sick was also a revelation that Jesus in his crucifixion and resurrection brings new life! My mother, Alta Rebecca Shenk, was the harbinger who with her literacy packet and her stories of Jesus helped to transform the Zanaki people. Occult and demonic emblems of power were burned and destroyed. Jesus was declared Lord, because they could now see that all powers were under the power of Jesus who had brought this knowledge to their village.

How could evil powers continue to be dismantled?

Jesus!

Education!

The coalescence of science and God triggered enormous energy as African societies and nations leaped forward into the twentieth century.

My mother had already helped the community to overcome other damaging misunderstandings and myths, one of these being that the milk from a mother's breast was bad for the baby. After we had first arrived at Bumangi, my mother began a medical clinic and taught that God had created the milk of a mother for the baby—it was good! She demonstrated this by breastfeeding me, showing the people how fat I was becoming by simply drinking her milk with no other food source. Soon the good news had spread among the Zanaki that God had created good milk for babies, and this greatly helped the health of the children.

My mother made many such contributions to the Zanaki society. In a fitting turn, the medical clinic would eventually be named the Alta Rebecca Shenk Clinic after her, even though she was not a technician and had probably never even handled a slide. The small medical team that Mother participated in worked together to establish medical ministries that blessed

The Alta Rebecca Shenk clinic. Rebeka Mirengeri Meso, oldest daughter of Meso and Wakuru, and Dulce and Karen Shenk Zeager, 2016.

the community in gracious ways. It was mutual hospitality wherein both Africans and missionaries became bonded in love and friendship.

And in this way the peace of Jesus was brought to Bumangi and the Zanaki people.

Despite all the good work my parents and other missionaries did, simmering issues in the Mennonite world weighed on them. When I was fifteen years old, the mission board delayed my parents' return to Africa for six months because my parents, along with other missionaries, didn't agree with the entire Mennonite Missions Polity, specifically the dress code that made Mennonites distinctive. The bishops and mission board felt deeply that there should be dress codes that distinguished the Mennonite missionaries from the society as a whole. It had taken about a decade to finalize this dress code, which included the plain coat, and a number of missionaries graciously challenged the polity. In due course, the leadership decided to show flexibility by releasing the missionaries to return to their assignments.

But this polity would be an ongoing issue—when my brother and I moved to the States in our teenage years, we discovered that we could not teach a Sunday school class unless we wore the distinctive garb for men. The prevailing thought was, how else would people know that we were born again?

We stumbled our way through this issue for many years. I had no idea at the time the hugely disappointing consequences this polity would have on me in my early twenties. But at fourteen years old, I was only marginally affected by the broader Mennonite mission context. I was mostly concerned that the new rules might require me to abandon wearing shorts.

Of greater importance to me at the time was my eligibility for a motorcycle license, so I laid my bicycle aside and cruised the byroads of Musoma at my pleasure. I roamed the bushlands seeking the poisonous mamba snakes, using their slim bodies as target practice for Dad's .22 rifle. I occasionally rode the cycle a mile to the lakeside where I could purchase fresh fish, and sometimes I would journey two miles to the grocery store.

My brother Joseph and I, along with a few other fellows, developed a couple of businesses, one of which we called the Bukiroba Fur, Trading, and Trapping Company. Quite often we jumped out of bed at 2:00 a.m. to scout the countryside for animals with good furs, processing the furs and putting the money in our savings for college. We had heard about an excellent college in the United States called Eastern Mennonite College. In light of that goal, we also captured bees for beehives and sold the honey for a good price.

Probably our most significant business was making tables that we sold to our African companions. Our father, along with a generous uncle in far-off America, provided several wood preparation machines, such as a planer and a band saw. My favorite machine was the lathe, and I spent many joyous hours working on it. A few years later, after returning to the United States for high school, I made a lathed bowl for a very special person I met in my sophomore homeroom.

But that was in the future. I was fifteen, and my parents had a year of home leave ahead of them, which meant another period of time in the United States, connecting with the Mennonite mission organization, visiting churches, and raising support. When they returned for this year of itineration, all five of us siblings accompanied them, occasionally giving slideshows for youth groups, telling them how wonderful our life was in

Africa. We went from church to church, telling everyone of the wonders of Bumangi, and the beautiful people we had come to love.

But one thing was different about this trip home—Joseph and I would not be returning to East Africa along with our parents and siblings. We would work the family farm in New Danville with our relatives and attend Lancaster Mennonite High School.

Still, I knew that I was not going alone. Jesus was my center. It was a new world, and I was excited to enter it.

Part II

United States: The Narrow Path
(1952–1963)

5

Cultures in Conflict

My parents' home leave was for a year, and a term of service with the mission board was for five years, so when my parents returned to East Africa without Joseph and me, we wouldn't see them again for five long years. I tried to be okay, but I wept alongside my brother, waving good-bye to our dear parents as they departed from the harbor in New York. I was sixteen, and Joseph was fifteen. We would be well taken care of by kind relatives and sure to write regular letters. We knew it would be a five-year separation, but we also knew that their departure was centered in a commitment to hearing God's call for our family.

You know, us Shenk children never debated or wondered if Dad and Mother were called—their calling was clear, and none of us would have done anything to disrupt it. Some of us were more enthusiastic about it than others. Those early teenage years in East Africa were very formative for me. I grew in my love for the church and was delighted that Jesus was my Savior and my center. The East Africa Revival was touching many congregations in Africa and North America with renewal and new life. I was formed very much by that movement.

I remember my dad telling me that he wished he could have taught more. He had become a man of work—he built churches and other necessary buildings. Once, he told me he thought he had built around thirty churches in East Africa. But when it came time to choose teachers and preachers, he was overlooked in favor of the more theologically trained missionaries, and there wasn't space for him because everyone saw him as a builder.

"My goals of becoming a teacher were never fulfilled," he told me one time as I drove him to the airport.

There was a real touch of sadness about that, but the church needed him to build, and really, his role as builder meant that he bonded quite closely with the Kenyan and Tanzanian people. But one thing he did, as I mentioned before, was to memorize the book of Hebrews, and he'd travel here and there, mostly in the United States but sometimes in Africa, and proclaim the book of Hebrews. He was quite an effective preacher, and he loved the Bible. And then he memorized Ephesians as well, which opened more doors for him. And I think in the end, anything he might have lost out on by not teaching, he gained during that time of his life.

During that same conversation, he told me something else that stayed with me.

"If the door would ever open for you to receive a PhD," he said. "Do it."

A part of me wished I was returning to Africa, but I knew that for the work God was inviting me into, I needed an education. Universities were hardly available in Africa, even literacy was scant, so getting a higher education while remaining wasn't an option. There really was no doubt in my mind.

What's interesting to me is that the missionary, revivalist culture we had grown up around in East Africa was keen on integrity, so when Joseph and I began living in Lancaster, we occasionally found ourselves butting up against a different kind of culture.

The first example of this came with our uncle with whom we were staying. He raised tomatoes for the family's cash crop, and the farm was on contract with the tomato processing factory. When our uncle said one evening that in the morning he would be delivering one load of tomatoes to a third party, something expressly forbidden in his contract, Joseph made it clear that he would not help. That would be breaking a promise, and he wouldn't participate in breaking a promise or a contract.

These were not simple operations—a wagonload of tomatoes was four tons. But I was entrusted with the responsibility of driving the John Deere tractor through the city, loaded down with tomatoes, and that was something I enjoyed immensely. I decided to help load the tomatoes—my brother was equally determined not to, and our relatives whose business it was to sell the tomatoes were dismayed.

Joseph, in his insistence to handle the tomatoes with utmost integrity, emulated the missionaries and the revivalists whom we had grown up with. In our home, we always told the truth. We were all relieved when the tomato contract was suspended because there were too many tomatoes to handle through the system.

I believe we may have inherited this integrity partly from my grandfather. I remember going with him to market when I was fifteen or sixteen years old, and he accidentally ran through a stoplight.

"David," he asked me. "Did you see what happened? I am a guilty man. I broke the law." He went on to tell me to look up and down the road to see if we could find a policeman to whom he could confess his misdeed. When we didn't find a police officer, we drove away.

"I guess there's no one there. I'm really very sorry for what I did."

I never forgot the honesty of my grandfather. This is the same man who never complained when his oldest son left the farm to follow Jesus' call. His life of integrity and gentle submission to the movement of Jesus in the lives of those he loved formed who I would become.

I ran into another cultural barrier at High Steel welding, where I worked several summers. I discovered that I was assigned to help prepare steel girders for an armory—I didn't want to invest in the military in that way, or in any way. I talked to the overseer of High Welding about it, and they respected my conviction, placing me on another job.

Still another cultural barrier for me became the pledge of allegiance to the American flag that we were supposed to say at school every morning. It disturbed me deeply to commit allegiance to a flag—I believed that making that commitment moved me into areas that contradicted commitment to Christ, so I simply refused.

While our parents were in the country, we could talk with them about these things, but once they left and we didn't have their counsel, I think we both felt a little lost, unsure of our direction. Yet both Joseph and I knew that Jesus was our rock—we never wavered from that certainty. I thought often of my conversion in that little Tanzanian church and the certainty of the call I had heard and accepted. This knowledge kept me moving forward with boldness.

The experiences on the farm formed me in positive ways, especially in regard to discipline. Joseph and I began milking at five every morning, and there was always the tomatoes, whose picking would not be delayed by any circumstances. But as I thought and prayed in those tomato fields during the long hot summer days of 1955, I began to receive clarity about my life, and I marvel now at how clear the calling was.

I knew I needed a community. This son of the Zanaki tribe needed a secure people. The second need I knew that I had was for a truth center. Those two realities were absolutely clear—I knew that without a community and a center, I would be taken apart by the new culture I found myself in. I was only fifteen when I returned from Africa to the United States, and I knew that I needed Christian friends.

In regard to community, I decided my father's home church, Millersville Mennonite Church, would be my church. Why? They had given to my parents the gift of faith in Jesus, so as a thank you for that faith I would commit to that congregation. Furthermore, I was dismayed by the spiritual dryness that prevailed among so many who attended there, and I hoped that Joseph and I could encourage spiritual restoration in that church. The revival in East Africa encouraged everyone to bring life to the deserts in their communities. We attended Millersville with an expectation of new life. And indeed that happened. There were more renewed people than I imagined. Within the youth group and the broader congregation, we found people joyously committed to Jesus, and they planted an enthusiasm for the church and its mission in Joseph and me.

In regard to my truth center, I knew that I belonged to Jesus. I would never depart from that call of grace offered through

Christ. Having these two commitments clear has meant that I have not floundered along the way.

I enrolled at Lancaster Mennonite High School for my sophomore year, and in one of my first classes I noticed a girl going past me.

"Who is she?" I asked my seatmate.

"Grace Witmer," he said. "But she's already taken."

Despite the knowledge that she had a boyfriend, Grace and I became friends.

I sent Grace a Christmas card during our senior year. She initially thought that I had sent a card to everyone in our class, thinking it was just me being a nice class president, but when she asked around and realized she was the only one, that made her stop in her tracks. Later on in our senior year, at the end of the school day, I asked Grace if she would accompany me to the senior class ice skating party. She was wearing a white jacket and snow gently fell on her dark hair. As I left the school lot, I called out to my friend, "John! She said yes!" That evening Grace was very gracious in helping me ice skate—in East Africa, we had no skates. She was kind, and that memory stays with me.

My family had come back from Africa in 1952. Grace and I eventually began dating in 1954. We dated for seven months, but the longer our relationship went on, and the more we talked about God's plan for our lives, the less compatible we seemed.

It wasn't that we didn't like each other—we did, very much, actually. And it wasn't that we didn't want to be together—we did. The issue that was hard for us was that Grace, while having a calling to share the gospel with people who had never heard, did not want to live overseas. She had a history of homesickness and wanted to remain close to her family. She was afraid of being so far from Lancaster, and that's what prevented her from accepting the possibility of overseas missions, where I was most certainly called.

It's a mystery to me even now, as I think back on it, how clear my calling was. It started on that bench in Mugango, and the older I got, the clearer it became. I was called to a life overseas.

It didn't make sense for Grace and I to say, "Let's continue dating without a real path forward for marriage and a life we can envision together." I couldn't do that, knowing that my life was called in a direction she could not go. We couldn't do it to each other.

However, Grace and I did plan one final hurrah. I persuaded Grace along with Miriam Wenger, the matron of the female dorms, to join with me in throwing a grand late summer dinner of African ugali (stiff mush). I had been elected the president of the class of 1955, and this would be a thank you to the class by sharing African food. I secretly viewed the party as a recruitment engagement for missions. It was a smashing success with fifty classmates. Until her death at 101, Miriam would often laugh at her goodwill in heading up that party—stirring ugali requires strength!

Before heading off to college in the fall, I stopped in at the office where Grace worked with a final note and a little handkerchief with a design of forget-me-not flowers on it. After being together for seven months, we called it off. It was a painful parting for both of us. Those were challenging times. But Jesus was my rock. My relationship formed with him in church during my younger days in Tanzania, during my early teens at the Mennonite school and watching my parents live out their faith, and solidified further while I prayed in the cow barn and in the tomato fields, working for my relatives. It was this faith that helped me through the heartbreak of parting from Grace, and my relationship with Jesus meant that when I left for college at the end of August 1955, I did not go alone.

By God's grace I knew the man from Galilee, and I knew my home.

I left for Eastern Mennonite College (now Eastern Mennonite University—EMU) in Harrisonburg, Virginia, even though I had an uncle who told me to skip theology.

"Skip the preacher business," he told me. "That won't get you anywhere. And this missionary work in East Africa? It's a waste of time."

He insisted, promising to pay my university fees if I would only become a lawyer.

"I'm called by God to be a pastor," I told him.

"Oh, you're missing out on an awful lot," he replied. But I gently deflected my uncle's plans and intentions for my life. I had a bold assurance of my calling, and a determination to respond to it.

I enjoyed my studies so much at EMU that I wasn't homesick. But I went through a dip, and some of the things I did seem so out of character to me now that it's hard to believe it was me who did them. I guess most of us do things for the approval of our peers, especially during those late teen years, and in this regard I was no different. I made myself generally obnoxious in the dorm, playing pranks that bordered on being mean. I was on precarious ground.

Yet all along, the gentle invitation of Christ to live into the calling he had for me never ceased. It was that calling, I believe, that led me through, even when my behavior wasn't always gracious.

Meanwhile, back in Lancaster, Grace was going through an evolution of her own. When she had been thirteen years old, she read the story of Philip and the Ethiopian eunuch, and that had been the basis for her desire to share the gospel with those who had never heard it. That's what she wanted to be about.

But not overseas. That was always her qualifier.

The year and a half I was away gave her a chance to think about why she was putting that restriction on where God might call her. She started sorting through it all and eventually came to the place where she could say, "God, I will go wherever you call me. You can call me anywhere in the world, and I will say yes." She had an overwhelming conviction that she should not put reservations on where God might call her.

But she did not tell me about her change of heart, not right away.

Then, during the Christmas of 1956, I came home from EMU for the holidays, and everything changed.

6

Joy at the Millstream

A friend invited me over for a Christmas party. I attended, along with my sister and my brother Joseph. As soon as I walked in the door, there was Grace, and I felt the same surge of wishing that things could work out between us, along with the knowledge that it simply couldn't—I was bound for overseas missions, and, as far as I knew, she would not leave the shores of the United States.

Someone arranged a Scrabble tournament at the party, and Grace and I were paired together. During the night of that Christmas party, I felt the same love and attraction for Grace that I always had, mixed with the same disappointment that we couldn't be together because of the chasm between our callings. But it was still a fun night, made even more so when Grace and I won the Scrabble tournament.

Guess what our winning word was?

Joy.

It was a thoughtful, reflective evening, with young adults catching up about the various directions their lives had gone since graduation. Christmas music played in the background, and there was a cozy, relaxed atmosphere in the living room. We were considering deeply where life was leading us.

I took Grace home that December evening, the car winding through the dark back roads, and as we drove she told me how her heart had changed. I was overjoyed at what I was hearing. She told me that she would go wherever God called her in the world, that she had removed any qualifiers or boundaries to the places she would go. My heart leapt inside of me.

Grace also surprised me by telling me that she had already registered for the two-year junior college Bible program at Eastern Mennonite College, so our paths would be rejoining again, both personally and academically. We decided on the spot to begin our relationship again, to further cultivate it and see where God would lead.

Several months later, in her parents' home, I put the song "O Star of Bethlehem" on her record player as we sealed our engagement with our first kiss. After that came a beautiful courtship for a year and a half, which was much longer than either of us would have preferred, but my parents were in East Africa, and Grace wanted to graduate from the college program before we married so that she could focus on her schooling, and then focus on our life together.

Those were special days.

My several years at EMU ended up being a good time for me to become conversant with the Mennonite Church in North America. This was in the latter 1950s, when racial issues were hot across the United States and the witness of Mennonite peace and justice was needed. I felt that the East Africa Revival Fellowship had an important gift to offer in the context of that era, and I was delighted to be invited for a gathering by an informal meeting of young theologians known as Concern. My appreciation for such renewal movements helped to broaden me and ground me within the Anabaptist vision. I felt I was positioned to encourage both movements by sharing their areas of common interest.

Another very happy development was the decision of the local Virginia district bishop to appoint me as a pastor in one of the mountain congregations when I was at EMU. There were only five families at the church, but preaching Sunday by Sunday was a most excellent way to give me on-the-job training as a preacher. Grace was commissioned to another congregation where she helped with the Sunday school program. The church I was assigned to was Mountain Top. Different students from the college joined me in this commitment, and I was affiliated with Mountain Top for the four years I was an EMU student. I loved to teach and preach. I find the preparation of a sermon challenging and exhilarating, and I love to expound the word of God. I especially enjoyed visiting in the homes of the people who lived on the mountain.

Then well into my senior year at EMU, something went wrong. One Sunday morning I completed the forty-five-minute drive from EMU to Mountain Top only to discover that no one was at church. I visited the homes of each congregant, and no one indicated the possibility that someone might be at church the next Sunday.

I discovered I had broken trust, and the Revised Standard Version of the Bible was the cause of this stone wall. In the RSV we read that a young woman will bear a son. In the King James Version a virgin will bear a son (Isaiah 7:14). In the Hebrew it can be translated either way. But in the mountains of Virginia it is "young virgin." In our classes the professors mostly used the RSV, but for the believers living within the Virginia mountains, the true translation is "virgin," and all other renditions were of the devil. I had used the RSV for my sermon on that fateful Sunday, and I grieved deeply. But no contrition on my part could reverse what I had done. I had preached from the Revised Standard Version rather than the King James Version. The sudden closure of this Mountain Top pastoral ministry was a tragedy.

My Virginia bishop took me into each home in the Mountain Top congregations the following week and pled forgiveness on my behalf. Alas, the damage had been done. My ministry to the mountain members had come to a close, and I learned as an aspiring preacher and teacher that a leader can make a mistake that will close the door on any further ministry. It behooves mission leaders to walk with humility and a teachable spirit.

It was not just the people who lived in the mountains who sometimes developed rigid directions. I sometimes did as well. In fact, one classmate said it this way:

"If you are a spokesman for the East Africa Revival, I would not view the revival as the way I would want to go." I had developed a critical spirit, which sometimes made it difficult to relate with me. This son of Bumangi indeed had a lot to learn in developing congenial relations and a softer approach. I needed a touch of God's grace, and God did not disappoint.

But not all was controversy and conflict. One beautiful dimension of my EMU years was the upper room, a prayer room found on the top floor of the men's dormitory. A cluster of us met in that room again and again for prayer, and a number of those represented became preachers and missionaries. It was within that fellowship that several of us began the practice of reading through the Bible yearly, and my preaching ministry grew out of a love for the Bible.

I have always enjoyed being a pastor and preacher—that commenced from my several years as a pastor at Mountain Top in the hills of Virginia.

Many students at EMU explored missions during my college years, and I enjoyed crosslinking with movements that were forming all across the country. Sunday morning prayer gatherings for missions encouraged me, and sometimes there were as many as thirty present. But we didn't meet only in order to pray: we wanted to cultivate relations between the college and community, and as opportunity developed, we conversed about Jesus. Remember how in Tanganyika, I or a sibling sometimes accompanied our mother in her Jesus-sharing walks? Now in Virginia several fellows went with me to the bars to share the good news of Jesus. It was quite surprising how similar the commitment to bearing witness to Jesus was in Tanganyika and in Virginia, and I was surprised at how well we were received in the community.

During my senior year, the senior class trip was to New York City, but just as the trip was upon us, I heard that Mennonite Central Committee (MCC) was in a cash bind, along with Eastern Mennonite Missions. I couldn't imagine spending my money on a trip when EMM needed funds to reach unreached people, so I donated the fifty dollars I had saved and stayed home, not going on the class trip. That was quite a lonely half week! But ever since I had been a kid and I gave away half of my bike money to missions, I had found great consolation in giving up things in order to further the work of Jesus abroad.

When the senior banquet came around, I originally decided not to purchase a corsage for Grace, by then my fiancée, and instead chose to donate the money to MCC. I believed it was another moment where I could give up something to help further the message and mission of Jesus. But a highly respected bishop pulled me aside when he heard of my plans to deprive her of a corsage.

"Remember Mary Magdalene," he encouraged me. "She gave a lavish gift to Jesus. Now is the time for you to give your fiancée a lavish gift."

Grace never forgot that corsage, and I have never forgotten the words of that bishop.

We enjoyed EMU immensely. Grace focused on Bible and I took a double major: social sciences and theology. We selected our studies specifically so that we would be equipped to teach emerging leaders in Tanganyika. In my mind, I was quite focused and certain about where my future would lie. I would return to Tanganyika, now with Grace, and we would spend our lives ministering there.

Every few months a team came from Eastern Mennonite Missions to recruit possible missionaries. They usually had a meal with us students who had roots in Tanganyika, and I was always an eager participant in such events. I loved Tanganyika and soaked up all the news about what was going on there.

As my EMU days were coming to a conclusion I invested further time in exploring African spirituality in the context of other spiritualities in books like Harold Bender's *The Anabaptist Vision*. I read it just as I was preparing to plunge into the secular, atheistic world of graduate school. In looking at his vision within an African worldview, it seemed to me that the absence of Jesus taking our place on the cross—in other words, the blood atonement—was a surprising omission. It is amazing to me how these concerns have never gone away. However, it was becoming quite clear to me that a gift of the Anabaptist vision was a clear commitment to Jesus and that all truths need to be tested through the litmus test of Christ. I was quite excited about visionary ways for encouraging fellowships between the East African revival and Mennonite Anabapist fellowships.

I was so keen about reading Bender when his book first came off the press that I forgot the cows had to be milked. My boss was not amused.

Significant missions opportunities appeared on the horizon. At one point, my favorite professor of church history stopped me at the water fountain in the EMU administrative center and asked, "David, what will it be after graduation?"

"A PhD," I responded.

The professor, I. B. Horst, cleared his throat and commented, "That might be all right. But remember God has called you to be a missionary and an evangelist."

Conversations like these helped me to become more and more certain about what my future would look like: specifically, I viewed my studies at EMU as preparation for a likely appointment as a teacher in the Mennonite Bible College forming in Nyabange. This solidified in my mind as the weeks passed.

But we must be careful about our certainties.

We must always remain open to the call of Jesus, as it is often unexpected.

On June 13, 1959, after a friendship, courtship, and engagement that altogether lasted seven years, Grace and I were married at Mountville Mennonite Church. Someone paid all of

our college debt, so we married with no financial liabilities—
we never discovered who the generous donor was.

In those days, the bishops decided on the décor and so
forth, and we didn't make a fuss about those sorts of things.

JOY wooden blocks to commemorate the winning word in Scrabble. Wedding
picture, June 13, 1959, showing David in his father's wedding suit and Grace in
the dress she made.

There were no flowers, in keeping with Mennonite traditions at the time, but we did have a male quartet who sang. It was a lovely wedding.

At one point we both gave a testimony from Psalm 118:23-24 (KJV)

> This is the LORD's doing; it is marvelous in our eyes.
> This is the day which the LORD hath made; we will rejoice and be glad in it.

We didn't have more than one hundred dollars in the bank when we got married, and for our honeymoon we rented a rustic cabin in a Pennsylvania state park, up close to Williamsport. That cost us about five dollars per day, and we did our own cooking in order to save some money. We stayed there for a few nights, and then returned to normal life.

I remember Grace and I stopping at a branch of the Fulton Bank around that time to put together a will, because someone or other had mentioned that when you get married, you should have a will. So, we walked into the bank and let them know what we intended to do. They brought out the bank manager, and he took me to the side.

"I presume you have a bit of money to take care of," he said in confidential tones.

"To be honest," I said. "I have about fifty dollars to my name." He seemed a bit taken aback, then nodded and quietly ushered us down the street to speak to a lawyer.

During the summer after we were married, we lived in the Lancaster area, renting a small place and working whatever jobs I could find. Grace expected a quiet and reflective home—I anticipated a lot of guests, mostly East African missionaries from EMM who were on home leave that summer, about twenty-five people in total. Grace's plan in hosting this group included about a month of planning, while my plan involved everyone bringing their own potluck.

Our differing expectations about the kind of home we would live in required some navigation, and as we grew older and served together, our seemingly disparate desires would meld into a combination of hospitality and sanctuary. In the end, during that particular summer, Grace and my mother shared in the preparation, we hosted the group of missionaries, and we had a delightful time catching up on the developments in East Africa and how the call of Jesus was transforming an entire region.

We also invited Grace's family into our home before we left for New York City. There were about twenty of us there, singing around the piano, when the floor of the cabin crashed! Fortunately, it was a simple cabin with no basement beneath it, so no one was hurt. My dad was an excellent carpenter and within a day he replaced the floor.

By the fall we had received and accepted a new appointment, heading to New York City for two years of voluntary service instead of participating in military service. At that time both Vietnam and the United States seemed to be considering the possibility of war. We were the unit directors overseeing sixteen young people who were also in voluntary service, sent by Eastern Mennonite Missions in their volunteers for alternative military service program. It wasn't the overseas appointment we both anticipated, but while in New York I could avoid participating in any violent conflict, encourage other youth who were trying to do the same, and explore furthering my education at NYU. We looked forward to this new adventure.

Our residence became 314 East 19th Street, New York City. This address has become a legendary guest house and crossroads for Mennonite young people in the city. It is now called Menno House. For us, it was the perfect transition point as we prepared ourselves for overseas missions, hopefully returning to Tanzania.

But in the meantime, we packed all of our earthly possessions into a U-Haul and made the move from our small town of Lancaster, Pennsylvania, to one of the biggest cities in the world.

7

A U-Haul to New York City

On the trip from Lancaster to New York I said to Grace, "This call to mission is the central drama of history, for it is God's kingdom that endures forever, not all the factories and tall buildings. It is the church that God is building. That is the heart of what it is all about. I am so thrilled to be part of what God is doing in the world."

Most of the volunteers at our center in New York worked in jobs approved for conscientious objection to military service. It was a significant ministry, one of those signs of the kingdom that the church disseminates around the world. As for the center, Grace was the coordinator of food and I was the unit leader, and one of my responsibilities included buying the food. Imagine how much food we went through, providing for sixteen young adults!

My first assignment was to paint the outside of our apartment complex. I dreaded the work, and often as I sat on a platform four floors high, the force of the sander would fling me away from the building. That job scared me!

When I wasn't painting, I was occasionally handing out hundreds of tracts, eager to share the good news of Jesus with the rest of the city. We even placed addresses on tracts and invited responses, and some readers sought follow-up conversations.

Soon after becoming settled in our Manhattan home, I walked to New York University and registered for my first course toward my PhD. I was grateful that EMM supported that goal—by the time Grace and I would complete our two-year commitment as volunteers with EMM, I had completed a master's degree that would go toward my PhD. We believed a doctorate would be helpful if we were to be training leaders. In the years ahead, as I launched into academics, I prayed regularly that if my academic studies would in any way detract from the Lord's appointment for us to serve in missions and evangelism, the door would be closed. But we prayed for open doors, if a doctorate in religious studies would create more opportunities. For us then the core reason for academic pursuits was to pave a way for mission. I decided not to go the seminary route, but rather engage in secular academic programs where I could focus on anthropology and sociology. In this way, New York University offered the right program for aspiring missionaries, or at least it seemed so to us.

Little did I imagine the ways that degree would open doors into the Muslim world for me for years to come.

When I think back on our two years in New York City, I'm filled with much joy. The team of sixteen who comprised the voluntary service community was a group with exuberant commitment, and we reached beyond our center. We held

The Voluntary Service Center—314 E. 19th Street, Manhattan, New York City, newly painted, 1959.

clubs for boys and girls, teaching carpentry and crafts. All of
the voluntary service members were involved in the local Mennonite churches, traveling up to an hour by bus or subway,
and I occasionally preached. We even developed a network
for Mennonite young adults in the city, a network that would
be a forerunner for what later became Manhattan Mennonite
Fellowship. It is evident now, in hindsight, that the center was
equipping a generation of Mennonite leaders; most of the volunteers emerged from that experience as leaders and teachers
within the churches in New York and regions beyond.

But something else important was happening. My involvement at the center formed my gifts in leadership, and young,
visionary adults looked to me as someone they would follow.
A significant dimension of that reality required maintaining
healthy relationships, and my peers at the center took responsibility to help me function in peacebuilding ways. I became
aware that effective leadership required listening, because trust
is developed when we listen. Without trust, I would be ineffec-
tive. I became aware within my soul that God's long-term plan
for me included visionary leadership on the frontiers of faith.

It was there that I also began to recognize the many ways
the gospel opens doors to introduce Jesus as the peacemaker
among many religions. I was increasingly immersed within
the ecumenical world and the world of storefront churches,
not to mention the evangelical world. I was finding that as a
Christ-centered Anabaptist, doors were opened in whatever
setting I served.

One of the residents worked in a gymnastics youth center
at Hell's Gate on the West Side of Manhattan, and a couple of
the fellows there came to faith in Christ, so I started meeting
with them on a regular basis. I caught public transportation all
the way out there in the evening and met up with them, having

a Bible study huddled among the freeways. It was incredible—no matter the weather, the temperature, or the time of year, we would meet.

Every so often I would show up, and the two fellows wouldn't be there. Standing under the bridge alone, waiting, wondering if I should go home or if they were simply running late, I'd often vacillate on whether or not I should continue meeting with them. On those nights when no one came, I'd go home feeling discouraged, and then the next week I'd wonder out loud if it was worth it. But Grace always set me straight, asking me what could be more important than helping two young men become disciples of Christ, even if it meant occasionally being inconvenienced? Of course, as usual, she was right.

It's impossible for us to always see the results of these seemingly small commitments, but thirty years later I was given that gift when I attended a meeting in the Bronx with a lawyer representing some churches there. Suddenly, the lawyer and I recognized each other.

"David," the lawyer exclaimed. "Remember those Bible studies in the Bronx?"

He was one of the fellows who had met with me for the Bible study under the freeway. And to think I had wondered if the meetings were worth my time. He had become a key leader within the network of Mennonite churches in the Bronx.

What wonderful memories came back to me in that moment.

Our daughter Karen was born March 15, 1961, toward the end of our time in New York. Her nurse, Trudy, was a Christian, and when complications arose—a heartbeat was not heard and Karen needed to be delivered promptly—this nurse passed the word to the network of Christian nurses in that huge New York City hospital asking them to pray for the delivery. A few hours later, Karen arrived safe and sound, our first child.

We were there for six months with her. Grace was perhaps a bit nervous about having a baby without any family around, especially her first, but we soon realized that even though we didn't have family close by, there was a Jewish lady we knew who Grace could call for advice, and there were other mothers we knew on our street who were glad to help. We both began to realize and experience how community can fill in some of the gaps that occur when you live away from family, and we also began to depend more on each other and even our children, as they got older.

As soon as Karen was old enough for us to take her for walks in a stroller, we would walk the streets of New York with her, sometimes taking her to the United Nations in the hopes she would pick up a kind of international flair and take on international interests as she got older. Even though our current assignment was in the States, our hearts still beat with passion for overseas mission work, and spending time walking beside the UN, a grand symbol of internationalist commitment, helped fortify my belief that we would soon be free to pursue our own international dreams.

As I had hoped, New York proved to be the perfect place for launching my academic goals. New York University had a credible anthropology department. Furthermore, EMM offered a one-year study leave after five years of service. I took full advantage of these benefits.

But not all was easy.

During this time there was quite a bit of unrest within the Mennonite community about wearing a plain coat (a specific dress coat for men), and occasionally I expressed my concerns about requiring men to wear distinctive garb. Sometimes I wore a suit coat instead of the plain coat. During my time at home in Millersville before leaving for New York City, one of the pastors told me that in my congregation the assumption was that I was a hypocrite because I wouldn't submit to the requirement to abandon neckties and wear the plain coat.

My brother Joseph submitted, and he received invitations to serve in the church. As long as I did not submit, I received no such appointments. However, in line with the teaching, I had eventually started wearing the proper Mennonite garb while in Lancaster, and this was one of the reasons we were given the opportunity that came up in New York City. But another problem arose later, after we were established in New York: I did not always wear the plain coat there, and my bishop was not happy about my inconsistency on this issue. But it wasn't only me: many Mennonites, especially those of us outside of Lancaster, were running into problems with this rule.

It was also about this time that Grace and I were eager to hear EMM present their plan for our first international assignment. Our two years in New York were wonderful, but our assignment there was drawing to a close and I was completing my master's degree. It felt like a transition was imminent, and naturally Grace and I hoped that it might be time for us to move to the assignment we had always been hoping and planning for: Tanganyika. We had prayed together for years about where in the wide world God might invite us to go, and in my heart Tanganyika was always the place I thought about.

Paul Kraybill, the director of EMM global missions, had a trip planned to New York, and he arranged for us to meet him at the train station when he was on his return journey later in the day. We met with him at a hot dog stand, and amidst the clatter of the 34th Street subway our director informed us what our future would hold.

"In regards to Africa," he said quietly, "that door is closed. Your bishop will not support you or ordain you, and we can't move ahead of the bishops."

The reason, he explained, was that in New York City I had worn a necktie, and over Christmas, Grace and I had put up a Christmas tree. Our bishop in Lancaster would not release us for missions because we did not abide by the regulations.

I didn't know what to say. I didn't know if I could speak. He went on to tell us that the mission board would appoint my younger brother Joseph and his wife to go to Tanganyika to eventually teach in the Bible school. And since the board had a policy against sending brothers to the same mission, the door was closed for us to serve in Tanganyika.

The message came to us without any warning. We were both in shock.

"What should we do?" I asked him when I could finally find words to speak. I was so devastated that I was surprised to hear that my voice worked.

He told us that if we were still interested in mission work, we could return to Lancaster and attempt to make peace with our bishop. There might even be a post for me to teach at Lancaster Mennonite High School.

The horrendous disappointment we felt in that moment is difficult to describe. As Paul departed on his train for Lancaster, Grace wept. I felt an incredible heaviness. We picked up our New York Times and returned to our apartment, astonished and grieved.

This was in 1961.

It surprised us how embedded ideological conservatism had become within the Mennonites we knew. For the conservatives, the issues seemed clear: born-again people needed to wear a special garb or sign so that the world would know that they were true Christians. What breaks my heart is that so many young people's faith crashed over this issue.

We weren't the only ones who had met the stern wall of Mennonite conservatism. My parents had also been denied a mission assignment for quite some time because of their preaching a revivalist message of salvation by grace. By this time, the revival that had taken place in Africa was touching a handful of people across the North American church, and the missionaries were the channels bringing new life in congregations when they returned to itinerate.

One such changed congregation met in the Bronx, and Grace and I joined that fellowship. The brothers and sisters there were also experiencing forms of opposition from the conservative camp, but as we shared the news with them, that we would not be appointed to Tanganyika, or anywhere overseas, their counsel was remarkable.

"Receive cleansing from any spirit of resentment," they encouraged. "You cannot hold this against the church."

One of the main emphases in the revival movement was to remain in the church that led you to faith in Jesus and preserve the unity of that church. If your church is dead, even more important that you remain and pray that God will use you as a channel for new life. We thought of all the saints suffering in Millersville under what we considered heavy-handed theology, and we began to envision returning to Lancaster to bring encouragement to the rest of the church.

It was at this time that, as the director of the young adult team in lower Manhattan, I was invited to participate in a late evening consultation that Orie Miler and David Thomas were having with several pastors whose congregations were pushing back against the conservatives. These men had full schedules, yet they drove 150 miles to the North Bronx to discuss whether the newly emerging churches could have a church council.

David Thomas worried that a church council would open the door for Mennonites to wear wedding rings, and therefore decisions surrounding conservative dress should be left up to the bishops rather than a council that might end up making long-ranging reforms. The meeting went until late in the evening and eventually disbanded without resolution.

Grace and I found ourselves among those in the center of these tensions—I was an EMU graduate attending NYU, someone whose influence might further erode the authority of the bishops. But I have to say that these bishops were gentle men, sincerely seeking the way. And several of them would find a way for Grace and I to enter a different door, not that far in the future.

After these meetings, Grace and I took the advice of our fellowship and repented of the temptation to join another denomination, such as the Christian and Missionary Alliance. This was counsel that was in harmony with the kind of counsel the revivalists were giving all across East Africa. It was the right path for us.

The fellowship and advice we received from that group in the Bronx was remarkable, and so important in its timing. They encouraged us to take up the offer of the bishops for us to return to Lancaster and for me to perhaps teach at Lancaster Mennonite High School, giving them another two years to decide if we could be commissioned.

It was just for a season, they reasoned with us. And we heard the wisdom in their counsel.

With the benefit of decades of hindsight, I can clearly see that these events were some of the best things that could have happened to us. Joseph was off to Tanganyika, and he was a better fit for the work there than I was. And would I have ever become involved in Muslim peacemaking without the conservative bishop who had the issue with neckties? Navigating these situations within the Mennonite world taught me the way of peace in conflict.

We moved back to Lancaster and joined a weekly fellowship of revivalists who met nearby. They continued encouraging us to follow the counsel to submit and wait for God's timing. I didn't realize it at the time, but learning the gifts of patient waiting and submission were valuable, especially when in the future we worked within hierarchical African leadership structures. It was there that patient waiting and submission would serve us particularly well.

Back in Lancaster, I taught the junior high Sunday school class in my home church as well as Bible and world history at Lancaster Mennonite High School (LMHS). Grace sold homemade cookies, and I sold fire extinguishers over the weekends to supplement our income. I began serious focus on a PhD from NYU. They would become two wonderful years filled with expectancy that one day our bishop would send us on our way as missionaries.

We had loved New York City, and we also loved Lancaster County. In terms of goals, the classes I taught as well as the education I was receiving were moving us in the right direction—that, I knew. We had one foot in the city and one foot in the country, working to build relationships between the two spheres.

A year after moving to Lancaster to teach at LMHS, there was to be an ordination for a minister at Millersville Mennonite

Church, and the choice would be made through lot. Within the Mennonite community, the lot was used to show that only God knows the heart of a person, and so when there is need for a pastor, let the Lord decide. This is how it happened at our church in those days—people in the church nominated those who they felt should be in the lot.

And I was nominated.

On the designated day, there was one Bible for each person nominated to be pastor, and at a designated time, the bishop prayerfully placed a slip of paper in one of the Bibles and placed them in front of the pulpit. Those nominated sat on the front bench, from oldest to youngest. This was high drama. For Grace and me, it meant that I might be chosen to be a pastor at Millersville Mennonite. The church was packed. After the sermon, each nominee chose one of the Bibles placed in front of the pulpit—one of them contained a slip of paper in it. In our case, seven people had been nominated, so there were seven Bibles.

Each of us, in turn, selected a Bible, then the bishop went down the line and examined each book to see which book had the lot. My Bible was empty. I would not be a pastor at Millersville Mennonite.

Although the lot did not choose us, the fact that we were approved for selection for pastor was enormously significant and encouraging. This meant I was no longer on the outside looking in—the bishop approved of me.

I wondered if our time to serve overseas might be drawing near.

I taught at LMHS for two years, from 1961 to 1963, and those were very good years. There wasn't any suffering on our part—we enjoyed it immensely. Several times during those two years, I took students from the school to New York City for exposure events where they could interact with various aspects of city life. These experiences were unforgettable for the rural youth of Lancaster County. I'm an old man now, but occasionally, when I'm visiting another church, someone will come up and ask me about the Old Testament course I taught at high school. They will usually remark that I was so full of the city, I wouldn't stop talking about the city, and that class somehow turned them around.

Toward the end of those two years, Grace was at her mother's house with our daughter Karen and she went out to get the newspaper. It was July 16, 1962. On the front page was an article announcing the news about Merlin Grove, an EMM missionary who had recently been martyred in Somalia. His wife had also been attacked but, somehow, she had survived.

EMM had entered Somalia under a United Nations Organization (UNO) trust mandate in 1953, with the emerging Somali government taking over more and more responsibility for the governance of the nation. The UNO required freedom of religion, and during the first decade, EMM served with the UNO, a good arrangement. A moderate form of Islam gained control of the political systems, and then things went seriously awry—this was related to the distribution of Christian literature as well as suspicions that baptisms had taken place.

Merlin Grove had been the director of the mission, and he had been stabbed to death. It was a shock, seeing people we knew affected in such a devastating way while following the call they had received to follow Christ to Somalia.

As Grace walked up the drive, a thought lodged itself in her mind, a thought she couldn't shake.

You'll take their place in Somalia.

At first, Grace wanted to push the thought down. Merlin's death was tragic, his wife's injuries grievous. Grace remembered the decision she had made some years earlier, that she would go wherever God would send her. The question was, "Has Jesus appointed us to go to Somalia?"

My brother Joseph used to say it this way: "David, when you are there by God's appointment, you can put up with an awful lot." It's true. Not all that has come our way has been good or easy, and not all that happened in our various places of service seemed positive at the time. There are hard things that take place. But we say "Yes" to Christ and his calling whether what is around us is good or not, because he turns it into good.

As soon as I got home, Grace shared the thought she had with me. We talked about it, prayed about it, and decided, for the time being, not to say anything.

We would submit. We would wait patiently.

Three weeks later, unbidden by us, the mission board approached and asked if we would take Merlin's place in Somalia. We consulted our pastor and our small group, and very soon we knew, without a shadow of a doubt, Jesus was calling us to go to Somalia.

Even during major transitions, life doesn't stop, and it was toward the end of this time at LMHS that our daughter Doris was born, on May 7, 1963. What a blessing! Two daughters! We reveled at the thought of two girls growing up together in Somalia. Sisters.

Doris would have her first international airplane ride at three months of age, when we left for Somalia.

We thought, in those days, that we would be serving in Somalia for a lifetime.

Part III

Somalia: The Open Door (1963–1973)

8

Praying People

With a rising sense of anticipation we prepared to go to Somalia. The invitation was a compelling one. I felt like everything I had done up to this point, every calling I had followed, had prepared Grace and me for this mission. And I would be returning to the continent where I had been born, where my father and mother still served. It all seemed to be coming together.

Though we would be going back to the same continent, Somalia was a very different place. When I had been born in Tanganyika, 80 percent of children died in childbirth. There were no schools. But during the first decade of my life, schools were built, medicine improved, and my parents, along with others, built a Christian community in the middle of Tanganyika, now known as Tanzania.

Somalia was different. For one, it was an intensely Muslim society. In Somalia, 98 percent of the people were illiterate, and due to the religious structure, they had very little interest

The Shenk family being commissioned by EMM to go to Somalia in 1972—
Front row, left to right: Jonathan, Timothy, Grace, and Doris; *Back row, left to right:* David and Karen.

in schools. Their primary concern was that children learn basic Arabic. That was all. It was also one of the poorest countries in the world, although Somalis did have abundant camel wealth.

The people were nomadic, migrating a thousand miles every year with their camel herds. They were a society which had never had significant engagement with the modern world. The leaders yearned for opportunities to participate in the fruit of independence, and they had asked Somali Mennonite Mission to participate in their vision.

Questions still swirled in our heads. For one, was it right to take two small children into a situation such as this? Small-scale military clashes seemed to break out every month between Somalia and one of its neighbors, and the country was becoming more entrenched in Islam. The missionary whose place I was taking had just been stabbed to death and his wife horribly injured.

Yet we received strong affirmation that this was God's call, and we were surprised at the deep peace the Lord gave us as we came to a decision to leave our home and go to Somalia. Of course we all remembered Merlin and wondered if there would be more jihadists, more martyrs. But our sense of calling made the question "How do you feel about going to Somalia?" irrelevant. The question was "Are we here by God's appointment?"

The answer was yes. Jesus, in his grace, had called us to this ministry among the Somali people. By God's grace we would serve with joy and thankfulness. We opened ourselves to the path before us, no matter what that path might hold. After all, that deep sense of appointedness had begun for me back in the second seat from the rear in the chapel in Mugango when

Camel caravan going past our home in Somalia, commencing their thousand-mile annual journey.

I was just a boy, the morning after I committed to following Jesus. I knew that I was called for this work.

We knew that if the assailant had known the love of God, he would not have committed this atrocity. We knew that our calling was to bear witness that God is love, and through the realization of that love, perhaps transform a community. We knew that Jesus was the embodiment of the love of God, that Jesus was the healer and redeemer of the nations.

The call had also become crystal clear to Grace. She never doubted our decision to go to Somalia, and her main concern wasn't with the potential for violence in Somalia or whether or not we would be martyred—her main concern was what would happen in regard to schooling for the girls. What kind of opportunities would the children have?

I was thinking recently about our time in Somalia, and my mind went to our son Timothy, who after graduating from EMU went off for a year and a half to northeastern Kenya to work in the biggest refugee camp in the world alongside the Baptists. It was a dangerous assignment—I sometimes wondered how, as someone who was a missions overseer and knew the dangers, I could encourage my son to do this work. He truly served on the front line, and at one point while we spoke about it, he admitted to me that it was at times dangerous.

"I've never told you everything," he once said.

But he went into that experience with the same spirit that we entered Somalia. If harm would come our way, it was all within the context of the call we had received.

It was Orie Miller, director of EMM, who noticed Somali camels outside his plane window as he flew from Addis Ababa to Nairobi in 1953, ten years before Grace and I moved to Somalia. As soon as his plane landed, he put together a team to explore the possibilities of starting a mission there. With rapid follow-up and United Nations support, EMM discerned that Somalia would welcome a development team.

Within a year of Orie Miller's flyover, a Somali Mennonite Mission team was present in Somalia, and the emerging Muslim state provided some religious freedom. As Orie had predicted, an independent Somalia soon rescinded that right, but by then the Mennonite presence was established, the first outreach among Muslims for American Mennonites.

Nearly ten years later, three young formerly Muslim men distributed Christian literature near the central mosque in Mogadishu, and that's when a self-appointed jihadist killed Merlin Grove and wounded his wife. Which in turn led to our arrival.

But the story of Merlin's death doesn't stop there. The government arrested the assailant, and weeks later there was a trial. At that trial, Dorothy, Merlin's wife, sent a letter to the judge saying that she sent no charges and in fact, she forgave the assailant. Many were surprised, and the nation was divided over the issue. They had never heard of such forgiveness. Others believed the jihadist's actions were justified—what forgiveness did he need from this Christian woman?

Many years later at a gathering of Somalis and missionaries, Somali friends made a statement asking Dorothy for forgiveness. In return, she asked forgiveness for anything the missionaries had done that was unkind or disrespectful of the Somali people. It was an incredible moment of redemption.

By the time we arrived in 1963 with our two daughters, Karen and Doris, two dozen Mennonite missionaries were engaged in Somalian education, medicine, and development, all serving under the invitation of the government. The Somali Mennonite Mission was a decade old and well established. I had acquired a master's degree in social studies education, and my assignment in Somalia would be to work with UNESCO and the Somali Department of Education in developing modern, secular education. Our plan was for an unobtrusive arrival because of the uncertainty around Merlin's death at the hand of a jihadist only one year before. But things do not always go to plan.

When we landed in Mogudishu, a city of around eighty thousand people at the time, it seemed to us like chaos, but to the Somalis it was delightfully energizing. We arrived in a DC-3 (these were the days before jets), and every time a plane landed the airport erupted with activity. We had been delayed one day in Nairobi, and I hoped that our representative from the mission had received our new flight itinerary.

We got to customs and immigration and waiting there for us was Harold Stauffer. It was so good to see a friendly face. The man at the immigration booth turned to Harold and, as

Karen and Doris with friends in Somalia—Johar Secondary School in the background, 1967.

he looked over our passports and papers, asked him, "Who are these guests you have today?"

"These people will be serving with the Mennonite mission," Harold said.

"Praise be to God!" the man practically shouted. "If you are with the mission, then you are praying people. We know you pray."

He stamped our passports, and we were in.

"The praying people have arrived," he said again, loudly and smiling.

I couldn't help but smile as well, marveling at the man's words. The Mennonites working at the mission had managed to make at least one impression on the community in Somalia—they were praying people. I imagined that these customs officials went home that night and told their families, "Guess what? Two more Mennonites have arrived, praying people, and this time they're teachers."

English classes had been established by the EMM team in Mogadishu. Those first students asked if we would meet them at eight that night and have tea with them.

"Of course. Wonderful."

So I met them at a kiosk by the roadside while Grace stayed home tucking in the children. We made small talk over tea, chuckling and laughing about some of the things I found remarkable about their country.

"Why did you come here?" one of them asked me.

"God called us," I replied. "God appointed us to come to Somalia."

"Oh, good," he said. "That's good."

His tone changed slightly.

"Hey, we're Muslim, okay? We don't need Christianity. If that's what you're about, go home."

And so we had a vigorous discussion, the kind of interaction I've never shied away from. This took place in the first twenty-four hours, and those kinds of conversations went on all the time, while we were there and then over the course of my entire life as I lived and learned among Muslim people. Theological dialogue never ceases among Muslims.

I think that's one reason I was so immediately intrigued by the wonderful people we met in Somalia, and I think it's why I find Muslims so interesting. They are a group that takes God seriously. They, very much like the Mennonites, think every aspect of life needs to come under the authority of God.

I had one such conversation around 2017 on a flight from Cairo to Istanbul, when I realized all five seatmates sitting with me at the back of the plane were jihadists on their way to Syria to participate in the Syrian war.

"Gentlemen," I said, once I understood who they were and what they were about, "let me be honest with you. I'm a follower of Jesus, and Jesus is the peacemaker—he has shown us another way, the way of peace. I encourage you to sit down and talk with your enemies."

We began having a debate at the back of the plane, and it became the talking piece of the entire flight. Some of the jihadists seemed to think, yes, perhaps talking would be better, while others said no, what they really needed was rockets from America.

"But you will never get enough rockets to end this conflict," I explained. "Only enough to keep it going. In any case, rockets are not the answer."

It was a rather rambunctious conversation, and at the end I told them that if they did not pursue the way of peace, the way of Jesus, in one hundred years they would still be fighting. Only forgiveness would bring true peace.

This is the type of conversation I have been having with Muslims for nearly sixty years, and they are almost always willing to talk with me about Jesus, the peacemaker.

These lovely conversations we were beginning to have with Muslim Somalians were important, and they took place within the context of what was becoming normal life. We were the headmasters of the new school, and a headmaster needs a new house (or at least that was the Somali way of thinking). So our house was more than adequate, even having indoor plumbing (which some of the neighbors had, but not all). We cooked by charcoal, so Grace had to get used to stoking the fire every morning, trying to find that one small ember that would restart the stove. We had to boil all of our milk and water before drinking it—there was no hot tap water, either. Grace used a charcoal iron to iron our clothes.

Within a week, we had all received Somali names: Karen was given the name Hoden, which meant "precious"; Doris was called Daheba, meaning "beautiful"; Grace was Nim'o (a Somali translation of the word grace); and I was Daud, the prophet. Later, Jonathan and Timothy were born as well, and their Somali names were Jama (a prophet) and Tawfiq (the one with the fear of God).

It was different from home, but we learned to live in that society. We would sometimes ask each other, "Do you like it here?" The reply was always, "Has God called us here?" We knew the answer to that: yes, of course, God had called us there, and we were in his hands. So with that attitude we could always answer with a smile, "Yes, we like it here. We like it here very much."

Doris, Karen, Timothy, and Jonathan growing up in Johar, Somalia, 1970.

One of the nice things about going to a country that was new to both of us was that it made the transition easier for Grace—both of us had to learn the country together, both of us had to learn a new language. Sometimes we sat on the rooftop, going over new words we had learned, talking about the society and how to live among the people. We did this together, and that made it even better.

Being in Somalia also meant going to Tanzania or Kenya for vacations, which was wonderful. I knew the Swahili language fairly well, and everyone knew me as the Shenks' oldest son, so they received me and my young family with great enthusiasm.

"Look," my Tanzanian friends would say. "They walked among us and loved us so much that they've come back."

Grace didn't have an assignment in Somalia, but she wanted to be involved. She held sewing classes for women, craft-making classes, and invited women into the home so that she could learn their language while also teaching English to those who were interested. She found ways to interact with people and went with the children into the village where they were welcomed into homes with Somali tea and hand fans to stay cool. She got involved at the school and the newly-developing church. In this way, she was very much like my mother during those early days in Tanzania.

Grace loved the people from day one. That I could easily see. And she carried herself with a purpose. She felt that what we were doing was very important, and that even though we couldn't share the message of the gospel openly in that culture, we could most certainly show people the love of Jesus, demonstrate that love, and if someone asked her about the love we showed, we could answer their questions.

Of course, Grace missed her family and friends, but the churches supported us with prayer and letters and Christmas gifts, and her family stayed in touch through the mail, which normally took a week to arrive.

We had a wonderful family of missionaries there in Somalia. God gave us new parents and siblings, Mennonites who worked at the mission and took us in under their wing. We loved that family, and eventually there would be forty missionaries there, the largest group at that time serving under Eastern Mennonite Missions. Somalia was where so many things were happening.

Wilbert and Rhoda Lind were two people who were important to us. They were the couple that directed the mission. They were hospitable and we have many memories of sitting around their table, sharing experiences, and eating gourmet food. Wilbert spent much of his time meeting with government leaders and asking how the Mennonite mission could benefit their society. As leaders, they provided vision and direction for the entire team.

We gathered together with the missionary team, in our different stations, once a week to pray, study the Bible, and share our concerns. It was wonderful. At its deepest heart, the mission was a prayer movement, a group of normal people who had dedicated their lives to prayer and to living out the call they had been presented with. What an honor, serving alongside the people in that group.

But it wasn't always easy.

We had to be careful the whole time we worked in Somalia. We had to consider whom we were speaking with and how we should say the things we wanted to say. The pressure came from both jihadist Islam on one side and, after the revolution, from the Soviets, who moved in and forced their political and atheist agendas onto the entire society.

This was a heavy load to carry, this constant vigilance. Eventually, after our time in Somalia, it took Grace and me some time before we could get over that sense of always being on high alert. It was illegal to propagate the Christian faith; however, students would frequently ask to study the Bible, secretly. We did not want to overstep our bounds, but it was amazing how there was ample space for sharing the good news.

Even in the midst of this, baptisms of new believers took place. The first three emulated the first Anabaptist baptisms in Switzerland: these three believers decided to baptize one another, so strong was the connection for those three to early Anabaptists.

For a full year, the congregation in Mogadishu had a Friday morning fellowship to discern what beliefs and practices should be developed within the Somali Islamic context. Some of the suggestions our Somali brothers and sisters made were surprising: for example, believers should stand to pray to avoid kneeling, because since we know Jesus as God the Father, sons and daughters stand to talk with their father—they don't kneel like servants. So, the best posture for Christian prayer would be to stand, facing our resurrected Lord.

As time passed, we formed a conference for the various fellowships, where they could send a representative. The first meeting was hilarious. Our chairperson was a missionary, and in the first session of what would eventually be a multiday event, our chair explained that the meeting would function according to Robert's Rules of Order. After an hour of trying to explain and demonstrate how Robert's Rules work, one eager Somali member raised their hand.

"Could we make our decisions the way that Somalis do? Where are Robert's Rules found in the Bible?"

Our chair finally agreed, at which point all forty of the members of the conference stood and shook their fists in the air and hurled shouts at one another in what appeared to be complete and disorganized confusion. A few minutes later, the Somali leader asked everyone to sit down, and he named each person who had been appointed a specific responsibility.

An anthropologist would later tell me that Somali decision-making procedures seem like anarchy to the outsider, but within the Somali context, shouting is the way decisions are made. We certainly experienced that. It was a lesson in the power of allowing cultures to operate within their accepted norms.

Our two boys were born in the cooler Somalian season—Jonathan in July of 1966, and Timothy in July of 1970. I joked with Grace that I had to go to Somalia to get our boys.

Jonathan was born in Jamama, Somalia, with Dr. Ivan Leaman delivering him. Grace and the girls flew to Jamama in a DC-3 and almost could not land because of the wet muddy field. They thought for a moment that they would need to return to Mogadishu. I went by land to Jamama to save money and had to wade the Juba River because the bus could not get through the mud late at night. Fishermen helped me to navigate the crocodile-infested river. When I arrived at the Mennonite Mission Center in Jamama I was covered with mud, and later we thought how funny it would have been if Grace's plane had returned to Mogadishu and I was in Jamama waiting for the baby.

Our son Timothy was born at Johar, Somalia, in the government hospital, since by then we were living in Johar, north of Mogadishu. Our EMM doctor at Jamama approved having the birth at the local hospital with Helen Landis Ali, who had delivered many babies in Somalia. The delivery became difficult and we cried out to the Lord to save the life of Timothy. I just wept and fell on my knees and prayed that the baby would live. The cord was around his neck and he wasn't crying at birth, but his skilled nurse Helen knew exactly what to do. We praise God for answered prayer.

Our family was growing, the girls were getting older, and Grace and I settled into our new life, living out our call. We went back to the United States for our first furlough when Karen was in first grade, and we were thankful that Karen could get in that year of learning. We all had a great year traveling around to various churches and catching up with friends and family. That furlough was exceedingly helpful when it came to furthering my PhD studies at NYU, but not without a near catastrophe.

It was my routine to go to New York on Monday morning for studies and stay in the city until Thursday morning, when I would catch a subway to Grand Central and then a three-hour train ride home to Lancaster for a long weekend.

This was before the computer age, back when everything was handwritten or typed.

I was deep into my New York Times, and at Grand Central I hopped the subway for the next link. Only then did I realize I had left my case of notes on the northbound subway, and nearly all of my PhD work was heading north without me.

I shouted to the Lord, "What should I do?"

I had already walked up one level, so I dashed back downstairs and noticed a northbound express was pulling into the station, so I boarded it. I watched as we passed the local subway, peering through the windows, trying to catch a glimpse of my work on the seat where I had left it. I hopped off at the next stop. My heart was in my throat as I stood on the platform, waiting for the train to arrive where I had left my work. I couldn't imagine beginning again. When the train came a few minutes later, I raced aboard and ran to where I had been sitting.

There they were. My notes. I grabbed my case and quickly got off.

Forever I will praise the Lord for that amazing miracle of successfully retrieving my PhD program!

Once we returned, the question of education remained a prominent one. All of the other missionary families in Somalia sent their children to boarding school as soon as they were school age, and while it wasn't something we wanted to do, we seemed to have no alternative. It was with great hesitation that we sent first Karen, then Doris, off to boarding school. By this time several mission agencies were partnering together for the development of a boarding school for internationalists. The school, Rosslyn Academy, was in Nairobi, Kenya, and continues today with about seven hundred students.

The tears still flow for Grace and me when we talk about sending the children to boarding school. But it was a wonderful place—the houseparents were kind and sensitive people, and the letters the girls wrote to us back home were filled with stories of the good times they were having. The educational program was excellent and the children formed deep friendships.

We recently found a letter Karen wrote to us when she was at boarding school, from October 27, 1968:

Dear Father and Mother

Are all of you well. I hope you are all well. On Friday night we saw slides. On Saturday we went swimming in the swimming pool. And on Saturday night we had company and us little girls ate outside. And for dessert we had ice cream with chocolate or butterscotch.

Today we had rice and curry for dinner. On Saturday night we ate flying ants.

How are Jonathan and Doris? I hope they are having a nice time. . .

On Saturday we went to the swimming pool, and I learned to do things in the swimming pool.

Love, Karen

We went to Ngong hills and took our lunch. I was the only little one to climb all the hills. The country was beautiful.

Also, there was this precious letter from Doris dated September 3, 1972:

Dear Mommy and Daddy,

How are you? I am fine.

I am having fun at school. I am going along fine with piano.

On Saturday Aunt Ruth took some of us children for a long walk. On the way back from the walk she told us to pick up some sticks because we were going to have a hot dog roast. When we came back we had the most wonderful hot dog roast, except that Prince (the dog) ate Bernice's hot dog.

Love, Doris

Last night we made pretzels. After we were finished making pretzels we had slides then we had hot tea. Last night for supper we had ugali.

While the girls were in school, Grace and I busied ourselves with running the school as well as hosting several conferences during that time in relation to Islam, Christianity, and peacemaking. Things moved forward in Somalia, albeit unobtrusively.

Or as unobtrusively as possible. Often, people in the local government would implore, "Please don't embarrass us." By this, they meant, *We want you to stay, but to make that possible, you need to function in ways that do not force us to take action.*

Another government official approached me and said, "I hear that some of our students are becoming Christians. It has to stop."

"When I came to believe in Jesus years ago," I replied, "Jesus blessed me with joy and thanksgiving. I can't destroy that gift! So, when students come to me and ask about my spirit of joy, and they want to believe as I do so that they can be joyful and thankful, what should I do? Is there a law against being joyful? What should I do?"

And the man laughed. "Oh, Shenk, you're doing good. Keep doing as you're doing."

On another evening during those years in Somalia, a student stopped by my niche and asked for a Bible study that would explain the gospel in ways that a Muslim would understand. As I stood there considering this student's late-night request,

I had a realization: I didn't know of any such book. I had nothing to offer.

I made that student a promise. "I will write that book."

The work I put into this idea became a four-booklet series known as *The People of God*, based especially on those Scriptures that the Qur'an already specifically cites as being revealed by God: the Torah, the Psalms, and the Gospels. Along with four students, we wrote this course imagining a Muslim reading portions for the first time. For example, we used Messiah as a name of Jesus rather than Christ.

Later in Kenya, we spent four more years developing the course, after which I met with a Muslim imam. I told him I wanted to write a Bible study for Muslims, and he was pleased. I asked his advice, and when the imam completed his critique and suggestions, he said he would recommend that all Muslims read the course, because, in his words, Muslims and Christians need to better understand each other.

We continued sharing the gospel as good news. As it says in 1 Peter 3:15, "In your hearts revere Christ as Lord. Always be prepared to give an answer to everyone who asks you to give the reason for the hope that you have. But do this with gentleness and respect."

So, that's how we operated all of those years in Somalia—with joviality, and love, and thanksgiving. It was interesting, wonderful actually, how by functioning unobtrusively, there was space for us, even in the strict Muslim confines of 1960s Somalia.

We were doing good work, but my vocational approach was challenged (and strengthened) during a visit from Orie Miller. He was in our home in Somalia to spend the night, and I was very pleased that I had gotten a diesel generator for the school I was developing. After all, I had been assigned as the

The People of God Correspondence Course.

director of the middle school, and we needed electricity. So I fixed this secondhand generator and it worked. I wanted to impress Orie by showing what I had been able to do.

Instead, he shook his head and said, "Mennonites always get the generators working. I am here to hear your five-year plan!"

I don't think he ever did go with me to look at the generators I had so skillfully used to create electricity, but his words made an impact on me and formed my administrative style. I began to focus more on goals and planning than on putting out small fires and focusing only on what was marked urgent.

But the rate of change in Somalia often made it difficult to think so far ahead. A constitutional amendment made it illegal to teach any religion except the true religion of Islam. Then the government commanded that Islam be taught in our Mennonite schools by Muslim teachers. This shift was

profound, and for EMM, facilitating the teaching of Islam was
a theological conundrum. Yet the young believers assured the
missionaries that full cooperation would build trust. After a
day of prayer and fasting, the bishops and board of directors
of EMM took action to accept the counsel of the believers in
Somalia and open doors for the teaching of Islam in the Mennonite schools. That decision was a significant move forward
in Christian-Muslim relations.

We believed the Holy Spirit was not bound. Faithful witness would continue whether or not we controlled the schools.

Of course, to me the irony was quite amazing. Here was
a board of bishops, some of whom had cited me for wearing a necktie only a few years earlier, now voting to approve
the teaching of the Qur'an in Mennonite-established schools!
Mission does indeed turn us in surprising directions.

Not only were we living joyful lives—we were also developing values that were a blessing to their society. A wonderful
high school. Programs for the community. Access to medical
care. And it wasn't just the Mennonite mission—there were
other organizations and agencies dedicated to improving life
for the Somali people.

While many of the things we did were planned, some
came about rather surprisingly. One such surprise was
uncovering the U.S. Agency for International Development
(USAID) windmills being held in the port. An article in the
Reader's Digest described U.S. government waste, including
these huge heavy-duty windmills stranded in Somalia. This
prompted me, along with Jim Shelley from our mission, to
walk up the harbor in Mogadishu and, wouldn't you know
it, there they were, disassembled and pieces all mixed up
together. These were heavy-duty forty-foot-high windmills,
and the head weighed a ton.

The article said it was impossible to raise windmills as heavy as these, and we needed windmills to pump up fresh water. The Somali government donated four of these machines to the Somalia Mennonite Mission . . . with no idea on how they were to be built or put up. The engineering fell to me, and the only instruction was a tattered paper telling us to form an A-frame.

I studied my high school physics book to think through lifting possibilities, and two USAID engineers drove fifty miles to where I was erecting the windmills to give counsel, but by the end of the day they declared it impossible to raise windmills without a crane; they drank their beer and headed home, wishing me well. Not to be deterred, I brought out our children's erector set and built a model windmill. Next, using a rope for a cable, I constructed a forty-foot A-frame, and it worked well.

Throughout this process, our team earned a reputation for engineering—actually, we were simply thankful that none of the machines crashed and no one was hurt. I believe God must have put angels on special alert. We raised four of these heavy machines and they served the SMM very well—USAID even sent several engineers to observe how we erected the windmills.

Actions like these were so fundamental to our mission, because we believed that good deeds were excellent and practical signs of the gospel. It was amazing that although it was illegal to propagate Christianity, the Holy Spirit was not bound, and we had many opportunities to share the gospel. Educated Somalis sometimes spoke of Mennonite values as desirable for a healthy society. Leaders encouraged seminars on truth-telling. Our two boarding schools brought together students from every clan in Somalia. This was tremendously revolutionary because in the traditional culture, these clans

Somalis and missionaries enjoying a remarkable reunion at Salunga,
Pennsylvania, 1985 (approximately 80 present).

were at odds. The interclan nature of the dormitories introduced interclan relationships, which meant our schools were
introducing an element of civil society.

As Somali Christians grew and matured, they took on many
church responsibilities. Somali believers baptized each other in
the Indian Ocean. The Somali missionaries were counseled not
to attend or participate so that we would not be personally
associated with these conversions. Later, when trouble began,
it wasn't the Muslims, but an atheist regime that sought to
turn us away. Yet the challenges of church meeting *ummah*
(the Muslim community) never went away, not even when we
used donor funds to build a modest mosque in the center of
the front courtyard of the secondary school.

Those early years in Somalia were characterized by hard
work, earnest conversations, and a constant desire to make a

difference in our community. We were responding to the call we had received, and it seemed good. We felt ready to continue in this way God had blessed us with.

What I wasn't ready for was a tear-stained note set on my plate in July 1969.

9

The Cup of Sorrow

In Mogadishu, Grace always planned the main meal for noon, and so on that day, July 21, 1969, I returned home for lunch. Just after I had sat down at the table, our assistant laid a tear-stained paper on my plate.

"Alta Shenk was killed in an air crash this morning outside Nairobi."

I burst into tears and walked into the bedroom to cry. The sorrow ran deep. My mother was dead. My parents, especially after us children had left Tanzania, had become an inseparable team, planting churches in the hinterlands, often on cycle or Land Rovers laden with building supplies. I knew my father would be devastated.

A quick check with the airlines showed that the only flight out of Mogadishu that would get us to Nairobi and then on to Shirati in time for the funeral had already left that morning.

Later in the day, while checking with the airlines, we learned that the plane needed to return to Mogadishu due to engine problems and would leave the next day instead. We booked the flight to Nairobi, which meant it would be possible to make the Mission Aviation Fellowship connections needed to get to Shirati in time for the funeral.

As we flew in the small four-passenger MAF plane en route to Shirati from Nairobi, there was a terrific noise sounding in intervals, a kind of intense clapping. We returned to Nairobi with fire trucks underneath us, the passengers greatly concerned about the state of the plane, only to discover the culprit was nothing more than the gas cap flapping against the fuselage. It was quickly repaired, and with great relief we continued on our way.

Mother was greatly loved, and if I hadn't known it before, I surely would have known it by the outpouring of love for her in Shirati. Some without bus fares walked significant distances so that they could be at her funeral. A thousand filled the church with ongoing waves of songs. Many of the people gave condolences, assuring our father that the crash was determined by God, but Father believed that pilot error caused the accident, not God. He asked for prayers that he would know the presence of God extending the grace of forgiveness.

"I can now say Jesus carries our grief," my father said, "for indeed, in my grief, I am learning to know this."

Alongside the deep grief felt by me, my family, and the community that loved my mother were theological questions. Most of the university students in my course on world religions thought God was responsible for such calamities, and these discussions were core concerns for my teaching in East Africa. Mother's funeral became an open door for theologizing core commitments of the Christian faith regarding God's sovereignty and our responsibility in the world.

Some years later, we passed through Shirati, where my mother was buried.

"Who takes responsibility for the very well-manicured grave site?" I asked Ludia Mbeba.

"I take care of the grave for Alta Shenk," she responded. "Alta Shenk was my dear friend."

Six months after Mother's death, Father came through Somalia on his way home to Lancaster, Pennsylvania. In our home in Mogadishu, after dinner one evening, Father asked, "What shall I do? I often said Jesus is our help in times of sorrow. Now I know that is true, for I am drinking the cup of deep sorrow. Jesus is my Savior within this valley. Now what?"

Grace and I both suggested that my father marry Miriam Wenger and return to East Africa. Miriam, you'll recall, was the widow of Ray Wenger, who had died of complications from malaria when I was a boy. She had been a mother figure for us Shenk siblings during the years that she lived in the United States, when we had been trying to adjust to life there.

We told Dad, "If you marry Miriam, we believe both the Shenk and Wenger siblings will be happy."

Shortly thereafter, my father Clyde Shenk and Miriam Wenger married in a quiet ceremony in Miriam's home in Lancaster. Bible college students from East Africa were surprised that a marriage could happen without the possibility of children, as in their culture marriage was about having babies.

As we anticipated, the marriage of Clyde and Miriam brought together the Wenger and Shenk siblings, and I believe that all of us children were quite happy with the arrangement. It was heartwarming to know that my father would not be alone. The tragedy of the air crash was transformed in special

Shenk-Wenger family Christmas at Migori, Kenya, hosted by Clyde and Miriam Shenk, while living in Kenya, 1973.

ways, and Clyde, Miriam, and their families have served in ways that have blessed many.

The plane crash in which my mother died was one dimension of tragedy—there were many varying dimensions that could occur when you were a missionary working overseas. Miriam's grandson Danny would eventually die in an auto tragedy in Nicaragua. This costly journey of faithfulness sometimes requires suffering we could never anticipate.

Yet with each dimension of tragedy comes a new dimension of grace and healing, both of which are central themes through all of our journeys. The emissaries of Jesus experience unanticipated surprises within experiences of grief.

One very special grace we experienced within the context of the tragedy of my mother's unexpected death was the bringing together of the Wenger and Shenk families, and the legacy of Mother Miriam's tasty Christmas cookies. Dad and Mother

Miriam lived in Migori near the Kenya-Tanzania border, and for a couple of years all the Shenks and Wengers living in East Africa would converge on their home for a few days of Christmas celebration each year, and those family gatherings were precious to me. To all of us.

Likewise, my university work with teachers provided an opportunity for me to spend an overnight in Dad and Mother Miriam's home in Migori. The combined love of the Shenk and Wenger families for Africa quietly opened doors for more opportunities as the years passed.

10

Muslims and Communists at the Junction

Things took a most surprising turn when Somalia succumbed to Soviet agendas. It all happened so quickly that it was rather shocking, actually. Atheistic benefactors from Russia banished Islamic society from Somalia, and the government declared Somalia to be a completely atheistic state. To reinforce this ideology, the communists killed the imams and forbade anyone from teaching Islam.

The revolution then commenced October 21, 1969, a straightforward Marxist-Leninist communist revolution. For these communists, ideology was the path into the future—the ideology of communism became their god.

Anti-revolutionary voices were silenced by the firing squad on football fields, and a terrible sense of fear descended on everyone in Somalia, a feeling that prevailed as clan leaders were killed by those holding atheistic ideologies. Then came an airplane crash over Mogadishu in which many people were killed, including imams whose duty was the teaching of Islamic leaders, and some felt it was God's judgment.

During these, our final weeks and months in Somalia, I gained a greater appreciation for truth-telling. In Somalia, this was another thing that was recognized as a Mennonite value—we counseled everyone to tell the truth, even when telling the truth might lead to difficult conversations with authorities or even arrest. We performed dramas for students and the local community that highlighted truth-telling as an important value. This was much needed in the Somali society.

We watched as major change swept the Somali society, as a Soviet-trained military progressively took control of the entire government. Even the camels were socialized, distributed among the people. The Somali language became the legal language of the land, in which they expected everyone to converse, and a special script was adopted, an alphabet unique to Somalia. Imagine the confusion of schoolteachers who now had to adjust the way they taught their students how to write, as well as introduce the first official alphabet.

It was so different than what we had grown used to, and the communist regime insisted there was no God. Ethiopia was having a revolution at the same time, and they were even executing children who they thought were sympathetic to capitalism. Forsaking the existence of God, killing children—these practices were not representative of Islam, not in the least. The people in both countries seemed to be losing their minds.

As communism took root, all of the Mennonite programs were handed over to the government, one by one. I lost my job, since a Somali became the new director of education within our program. We and all the missionaries we worked with cooperated in all ways possible with the authorities, not wanting to jeopardize our ability to remain or lose what was accomplished as we and Somalis of good will had worked together for nearly two decades. We had earlier cooperated with nationalization and with teaching Islam in our schools, and that spirit had earned us great trust.

But what would become of us now? What would the communist regime think of the Mennonites and our programs?

As the communist revolutionaries inaugurated destructive rampages, I went to the United Nations offices one day. "How do you maintain hope when so much of what you have developed is ruined?" they asked me.

"We live in the hope of God bringing about the formation of the city of God where righteousness and justice prevail. That keeps me going."

I said the same when many of our Somali friends asked why I cooperated by handing over personal belongings that we owned. During this time, when everything was being turned over to the government, an officer came to take my scooter. Even though he could not ride it, it must be handed over, so I drove it to his office and gave him the keys.

Then I walked home. I suppose by sundown many had heard of a Mennonite teacher turning over the keys of his scooter to a communist officer. Many of our Somali friends asked us why we were cooperating. I always had the same response:

"We are guests in Somalia who want to serve in ways that the Somali people ask us to serve. As you know, I am a follower of Jesus, and he has taught us to serve one another. We will serve as long as you request and then when our time has come to leave, we hope to leave in a way that blesses us and blesses the entire Somali nation. I have enjoyed the scooter. Now it is time for the scooter to encourage someone else."

Even though the nationalization of all schools meant I had no job (a Somali now occupied my office), I hoped that a long-term vision might be unfolding for Grace and me, where I could join the university that was emerging and help to form it into a place that focused on peace studies. So it was with great expectation that I attended a meeting with the communist university president. Could it be that a long dream of bringing peace studies into the academic world was unfolding?

But in our meeting I quickly realized the communist president of the university was championing atheism. I was astounded and deeply disappointed. He was proclaiming atheism as the way forward for the country, and there would be no room for religious studies of any kind.

"We are creating a Marxist-Leninist university," he told me. "All professors will be atheists. Muslims do not qualify. Neither do Mennonites, for you are believers. Go to Kenya. They like God there. You will find a job in Kenya; however, here, in Somalia, there will be no opportunity for you to teach religion. Our direction is clear—Islam has destroyed the good values of our people. We have had enough religion. Now? We want liberation."

That door closed.

I left the president's office musing on the irony of it all. I had gone to New York University, a secular school in the United States, to study world religions in order to teach in a Somali university, only to discover that only atheists may apply.

Grace and I considered appealing directly to the president of Somalia—after all, two of his children had studied in our

Mennonite schools. But after a friend found his way into the security file, he reported back that he would strongly counsel us to leave the country.

We were perplexed, and it was with sad hearts that we began to pack for our next adventure in missions. We decided to leave Somalia in January and wait in Kenya for further discernment. We were two of the first EMM missionaries to leave, and over the next few weeks the transition from an American to Somali director of education in our schools went smoothly.

During the next six years, the Mennonite appointees were reduced year by year until all the Mennonite appointees at the school were replaced by Somalis willing to proclaim atheism as their worldview. Eventually, the message solidified: Muslims and Christians need not apply. A number of our Mennonite team had invested much in helping the secondary school become an excellent institution, but the decision of the Somali government to hand it over to revolutionaries would eventually destroy the school. It became a calamity. Bright young people were bereft of any possibility to acquire a good high school education anywhere in Somalia.

I grieve for Somalia now, full of such wonderful, wonderful people. Why, oh why, have they gone in the direction they have gone? It's volatile, and it keeps escalating. We felt that was an important part of our calling there—breathing peaceful alternatives into their society. And Somalis had let us know that is what they wanted, what they needed. The gift of respecting the one you disagree with. The gift of forgiveness. The gift of conversations.

We found ourselves with two options: leave East Africa and the ministry there, or reengage with a new focus, in a new location. Our EMM board requested that we leave East Africa and return to the United States to serve in the U.S. office. But we felt strongly that our calling to the Islamic world was not yet complete, so EMM gave us their blessing to remain in Africa and try to discern a way forward there.

Harold and Barbara Reed were the directors of Somalia Mennonite Mission, and as we enjoyed a last evening dinner with the Reeds, they asked what our hopes were for next steps. We said our first step was to transfer from Somalia to Kenya, a nation that was mostly Christian and constitutionally committed to religious freedom. Kenya and Somalia were adjacent countries, but Somalia was one hundred percent Muslim; in fact, we had been informed at one point that Somalia was the only country wherein the blood of every citizen was Muslim.

With robust hopefulness, we trusted God would open doors once we arrived, doors with ready access between Kenya and Somalia, a country we still loved. We told the Reeds that we were praying for open doors in three specific ministries: first, that we could join with Kenyan Mennonites in developing Mennonite churches in Kenya; second, that I could join the faculty at Kenyatta University College to teach courses on world religion and peacemaking; and third, to develop Muslim ministries in East Africa.

The night before we left Mogadishu, Somalia, in 1973, a young woman wanted to be baptized on New Year's Eve. What a moving request! As many as possible gathered in our small bathroom so she could be immersed in our tub at her request. When she came up from the water, there were tears in my eyes: joyous at her obedience to the call of Jesus on her life, but perhaps also a bit sad at what we were leaving. Still, what a glorious entrance into the New Year, for her and for all of us. This was the first woman we knew of to be baptized in

Somalia, and it seemed a special grace that we could witness it before we left.

Ten years had passed since we first arrived in Somalia, and there we were, back in the Mogadishu airport, this time leaving Somalia for good. Grace and I had hoped for a lifetime of engagement with Somali Muslims, for a lifetime of friendships and teaching and baptism, but now the doors for ministry within Somalia were closing.

It was a time of grief for us over a mission cut so very short.

During the next month, we were amazed by how events unfolded. Within a few days of our arrival in Kenya, we received invitations for ministries in harmony with the three ministry areas we had hoped for. We also received counsel on the various regions of the city of Nairobi where the most Muslims lived, and we decided we would focus on the Eastleigh area.

As a consequence, we settled into Kenya and immersed ourselves in all matters Kenyan, beginning an entirely new engagement on the continent. Kenya was an excellent show-and-tell of how thriving Christian churches and bustling Muslim communities could coexist. In Kenya, our family would experience both tragedy and hope—our four children would immerse themselves, living and serving in both Christian and Muslim worlds.

Ministries flourished.

They would be good years.

Part IV

Kenya: Unexpected Possibilities
(1973–1979)

11

Welcome to Kenya

Within a month of arriving in Kenya, we were involved in all three of the dimensions we had spoken about with the Reeds, but in one of those areas, EMM rebuked me. I had spoken with the Kenyan leaders of the Mennonite church in Kenya and after a few conversations they asked if I would start a church in Nairobi. At that point, there were Mennonite churches in Kenya, but none in Nairobi.

But having a missionary plant and lead a church went counter to EMM's mission, in which all church plants were led by local leaders. EMM felt churches should be planted by Africans, but we felt both working together could be helpful.

I asked EMM, "What should I do? Should I obey you or the Kenya Mennonite Church, who is asking me to get involved? Whom should I submit to?" I had a strong desire to be involved, and the fact that the local people invited me to do it felt like a compelling call.

When I put it like that, EMM relented. "Go ahead. Follow the local church's counsel." This was a big step into granting autonomy to local congregations, even if what they desired at first went against our policies or western sensibilities. We were challenged to constantly reexamine what lay at the core of Christian faith, and what issues or policies were based in Western culture.

Because of this development, from very early on, Grace and I were heavily involved in the local church in Nairobi.

Before we had even left Somalia, one of the most crucial conversations I had through letters was with Professor B. W. Andrzejewski, a Polish anthropologist with special focus on Somali studies at the University of London School of Oriental and African Studies, about the best way to introduce Jesus to Muslims. I just couldn't see any cracks in the order of Islam—it was a self-propagating ideology that was coherent and made sense, so why in the world would a practicing Muslim open the door to consider something as strange as the Christian religion?

What was the key?

He told me something that completely shaped our approach in East Africa: the Sufis are the way into Islam. This is because of their mystical, spiritual approach. The Sufis are on a quest to know God, to have the blessing of God, to be identified as intercessors, and to be a community of peace. Islam in general says there is no possible way of knowing or meeting God—he reveals his will, but not himself. There is no incarnation, no God who meets us. There is no God appearing within a burning bush. Messengers might come, but they are simply that: messengers. Those messengers are never God himself.

I believed the Sufi quest was fulfilled in Jesus Christ, and that's what my friend was insinuating. The gift of the gospel in this setting is the good news that God has appeared, that God has come and lived among us. That's precisely what the Sufis seek! Besides that, Sufism is peace-loving, peace-seeking.

So, shortly after arriving in Kenya, I wrote a substantial paper on Sufism as a spiritual movement that is fulfilled in Jesus as revealed in the book of Hebrews. We decided to put the findings of that paper into practice. The first step was to find a Sufi community and to become a Sufi-like community ourselves, with one core difference: Muslims place the Qur'an at the center, while Christians place Jesus at the center.

In search of a place to embody this vision of working among Sufi Muslims, Grace and I climbed in Don Jacobs's Peugeot and drove from one side to the other of Eastleigh, a place noted for its terrible congestion. It was also a primarily Muslim district, about twenty blocks from one side to the other, and filled with mostly Somali Muslims who had fled the communist takeover of their home country. And the rumors we had heard were true: it was an exceedingly congested area where new refugees congregated, the houses full of people, the streets crawling with traffic. Fortunately, I had a little Honda 80cc motorbike, which meant I was never stuck in traffic—I just weaved my way back and forth through the gridlock.

The smile of God on our vision was apparent from the beginning, especially the aspect of our dream that had to do with living in a Muslim area of Nairobi. Amazingly, we discovered on Eighth Street the construction of a building with five apartments and a vacant lot on either side of the apartment building. There was nothing else like it in all of Eastleigh. Also surprising was that a mosque was right at the heart of Eastleigh, across from the new apartment complex. Grace and I had a vision for developing a center right there at the junction of Eighth Street where Muslims and Christians could come together!

Of course, it had to be approved by Eastern Mennonite Missions and the Kenya Mennonite Church, as well as the Tanzania Mennonite Church. We were given the green light to find the funds and move forward with purchase of the property. Getting that stamp of approval required a five-hundred-mile trip to Tanzania headquarters. In spite of the complexities, the church was delighted and the people of Eastleigh were eager.

The first step was securing one of the apartments, so I asked one of the workmen if he could tell us who owned the building. He gave me the landlord's information, and we met.

"I have a family of four children," I said, "and we'd like to live in Eastleigh. Is this a possibility? Are any of the apartments still available?"

"There are five apartments," he said. "And all of them are available. But you don't want to buy just one—it would be better for you if you owned the whole building, and then you could control who your neighbors are."

What he said made sense, especially if we were to turn the neighboring plots into a community center. But that was a huge commitment. I wasn't sure what to say.

"You're a man of God, I'm a man of God," the man said. "Let's work this out."

Before long this Christian businessman promised right there on the street to sell us the property. We would work out the details. He had just built this investment property, yet he gave it up because he was a man of God and I was a man of God. It took some time to work out the finances, but we had a clear commitment.

But there was a roadblock in the development of this Eighth Street junction. To develop the kind of center we envisaged required all three urban plots: the apartment building and the vacant plots on either side of it. All needed to be purchased on the same day, and while I had commitments for the apartment and one of the neighboring plots, for at least a year the Kenyan representative could not make contact with the owner of the third plot.

Or, as it turns out, the Kenyan representative *would* not make contact with the owner.

I rode my cycle through the city to this address many times, day after day, staring at the three plots of land, dreaming of what could be done there to help the Eastleigh people. On one of my many cycle rides, a young man motioned for me to join him behind a wall, and when I did, he told me that his father owned the property and the director I had been speaking with and inquiring with was blocking me from contacting him. That was an interesting piece of information, but it made sense in light of the continued excuses this director had always given as to why I couldn't talk to the owner. But even more fascinating—the young man gave me the address where his father lived . . . in Coventry, England.

It just so happened that we had an upcoming home leave scheduled to the United States, and we traveled through England, so once we were in London, I placed my dear family in a hotel close to a park while I scooted on a train to Coventry. The trip would take most of the day.

I arrived at the address the young man had given me and I knocked, and the door opened. A Sikh stood there in front of me.

"What brings you to Coventry?" he asked graciously. "Is it the Eastleigh property?

"Yes."

"How much will you give me for it?"

I said a dollar amount.

"Deal."

I suppose his son had informed him that I was on my way, and he was prepared to relinquish the property. It all seemed to happen so fast, once I had finally come face-to-face with the person in charge of making decisions.

Once we had all three properties secured, it was sufficient space to build a community center, and our vision in Eastleigh was well on its way. All that remained was to secure the funding for the transaction, about half a million dollars. On our return flight, we flew through the Netherlands so that I could meet with Bread for the World, an organization that provided grant funding for hospitals and other community-based projects. I let them know I'd be in town and would like to meet with their decision makers about a project in Nairobi, Kenya. They agreed to meet with me.

I stopped off for the afternoon, once again setting up my family before heading to the meeting.

"Do you know Dutch?" the representative asked me.

"No."

"How can you say you don't know Dutch when you come from the area of the Pennsylvania Dutch?"

"Yes, that's true."

"Shouldn't you know the mother tongue?"

"Yes."

"Don't you think you should know Dutch if you're going to come here and ask for money?"

I wasn't sure what to say.

"This project you've brought up, we're quite excited about it," he said. "But there's one word there that makes us uncomfortable. One issue. 'Evangelize.' Just drop that word. Go ahead and do your evangelization, but don't put it in your application, and I expect we'll have money for you."

And that was what we needed for the project: a simple change in terminology on the loan application. When I returned to find Grace and the children, I was eager to give her the good news. We would be acquiring the Eastleigh apartment building and the plots on either side.

We rejoiced in the providence of God.

The truth is, the vision was our vision, together. It was always both of us. We were both committed to it.

And God prospered that vision—Eastleigh contained every language group in Kenya, and most people were Muslims. The people moved back and forth using the facilities in every way, every day. I have always felt like it is a sign of the kingdom where the languages of many nations meet and greet one another.

There were other centers in Nairobi, but in terms of the Kenya Mennonite Church or Muslim ministries, Eastleigh would become a hub. We were eager to complete the Eastleigh Center and begin our work among the people there. As soon as the contract to purchase could be sealed, we moved into Eastleigh with our four children, who were becoming teenagers.

The street where all of this happened, Eighth Street, was a dead-end street, so for our sons, Eighth Street became the soccer center for that section of the city. Furthermore, the daughters of the imam became acquaintances and friends with our girls. Our entire family quickly became part of the fabric of Eastleigh, as did the Christian residents of the center.

As we became more familiar with our children's friends, we asked them what urgent needs they had. What is the first thing we could do to benefit our community? Unanimously, they said a reading room was needed—entire families lived in one-room apartments, with no space for the children to study apart from the noise and commotion of the rest of their families.

So we turned the rooftop into a reading room, and the children's grades all across Eastleigh improved. It was the first step in helping children move away from poverty, and within four years we were able to negotiate grants for the Eastleigh Fellowship Center, which attracted hundreds of students a day. The reading room continued to be an important aspect of the center.

Of course, such projects require funds, and even our children got in on the act of raising money. Our youngest, Timothy, who was four years old, went door to door collecting money for the building of more adequate facilities.

Looking back, I can now see how our years at Eastleigh were nudging us even further in the direction of Muslim-Christian relations. We sometimes invited the imams and sheikhs to tea or food on one of the rooftop terraces. In those dialogues, the conversations became centered in Jesus, and walls came down.

Eastleigh Fellowship Center with Joseph Ngarama. The acquisition of this building was a miracle, 2012.

A noteworthy basketball team, the Menno Knights' Gym, in the Eastleigh
Fellowship Center where our family lived for four years. Girls teams have also
been noteworthy.

The mosque across the street from the Eastleigh Fellowship Center.

I found myself becoming more and more interested in hosting these kinds of forums. That Eastleigh Center became a center for dialogue and conversation.

During a recent visit, I was delighted to see over a hundred Muslims and Christians participating in conversations about Jesus and his mission at the center. I was asked to speak on the topic, "Who is Jesus?" I simply shared vignettes from the life of Jesus and then asked, "Who is this man?"

A lively discussion ensued. But it's hard to imagine this kind of conversation ever happening, or at least me playing a part in it, without those years we spent in Eastleigh.

I recall a feisty splinter group off of mainstream Islam that met close to our community center, and the sheik of this group would stand diagonally across the street from where we lived and he'd blast away with his megaphone, warning people about us, declaring that our goal was to convert them out of Islam. He was very anti-Christian.

One day I walked over to him.

"Sometime," I said, "we ought to sit down and talk, instead of you just standing over there shouting."

He seemed agreeable to this.

"Why don't we have tea together," I suggested. "You bring your disciples and I'll bring mine. You can share what drives your vision, and I'll share ours."

"Dr. Shenk," he said, somewhat surprised. "That's a very good idea. Let's do that."

So, one evening we met on the rooftop at one of the nicest restaurants and shared a goat feast. And there we sat, ten of them, ten of us, talking about this Jesus who had so captivated us.

This sheik would eventually be the Muslim I chose to critique the final revisions of *The People of God,* and he was incredibly pleased that I would trust him so much. If you'll remember, *The People of God* was a booklet series first conceived in Somalia and then furthered in Kenya. For many years, the center in Eastleigh circulated a thousand of those courses a

David and his assistant, Yurup Halima Jamma, at the Nairobi office in Eastleigh, sending out the People of God study course to students, 1978.

year with hundreds coming to faith in Jesus the Messiah. Even today, other churches and agencies are carrying *The People of God* forward, using it in all manner of ways. It has been translated and printed in about thirty languages, with several used in radio or on the internet. And it all began with a late evening knock at our door, with a Muslim student requesting a simple Bible study that would appeal to Muslims. And it came to completion with my friend, this sheik who was at first almost militant in his opposition to our presence.

And again I am reminded: follow the call. Say yes to Jesus.

The mosque we were neighbors with in Eastleigh was a Sufi mosque, and because the Sufis believe in divine healing, the door was open for me and my Kenyan colleagues to attend, from time to time, to pray for a rather sickly imam in his home. This was one of the reasons we were so well-received in Eastleigh—there were Sufis who yearned to know Christ as revealed in the biblical book of Hebrews. Jesus as intercessor is particularly attractive to Sufis. I was amazed—we had arrived in Eastleigh from Somalia on the same street as a Sufi imam who was sickly and welcomed prayers to God in the name of Jesus, and so we were praying in Jesus' name for his healing.

These were not the results of our own plans. God had clearly gone ahead of us, even as we were being forced to leave Somalia.

Again, I was reminded of the power of saying "Yes" to Jesus.

Within a year of our family arriving in Eastleigh, other families and single people developed interest in emulating our approach to Muslim communities, so another team was developed in the remote desert lands of Northeast Province in Kenya. These communities being built up were centers of peace where people could flee in times of danger, and as a response to this need for peacemaking, a prayer team was formed within the center whose ministry was for the peace and healing of the Somali people and other ethnic groups as well.

Jesus the healer appeared in visions in these ministry centers, and in due course these appearances of Jesus happened with increased fervor. I have heard stories of imams in Ethiopia who met Jesus in their dreams and would then enter mosques and lead whole congregations of Muslims into a commitment to Jesus. What made these movements even more remarkable was that they were thoroughly indigenous and occasionally accompanied by intense suffering imposed by forces who opposed the message of grace the people of God proclaimed.

Meanwhile, my own siblings were becoming scattered, not only in the United States, but around the world in Somalia, Tanzania, and Kenya. My brother Joseph taught at the Bible college in Nyabange, my brother John was teaching in a Kenyan high school, my sister Anna Kathryn and her husband, Omar, eventually served in Zambia and in a high school run by the churches in Musoma, Tanzania. Our youngest brother planned a visit to East Africa where our parents were living on the Tanzania-Kenya border and beginning churches in Kenya. We delighted in the joys of living and ministering in East Africa.

Kenya wasn't this end-of-the-earth kind of place, either— it was ideal for children and families. There were abundant mountains for hiking, and one weekend our family drove fifty miles to Lake Naivasha. There were six of us in our Toyota Corolla along with an old-fashioned tent, food, and cooking utensils. We had been duly prayed for by our charismatic neighbor as we left our home.

During the night at Lake Naivasha it rained so heavily that our tent became soaked inside and out. Everyone was packing up to leave, including us, and eventually we were the only ones left on the lake, so we decided to go for one last spin in the little boat before heading out. As we enjoyed the beauty around us, our motor failed.

We had no oars.

And then, to make things even worse, a hippo appeared in the water. As we watched, the hippo disappeared under the surface of the water, and when it surfaced, it was a bit closer. Again, it went under and emerged even closer.

We prayed, and I continued pulling the rope to get the motor started—any place with an angry hippo is the wrong place to be! These fast-moving animals can be quite aggressive when they feel their territory is being infringed on. I kept glancing over at Grace, and I could tell that she understood the gravity of our situation. I pulled the rope again. Still no luck. Fortunately, the children seemed oblivious of our danger.

Finally, one of my tugs on the rope brought a timid ignition to the motor. We praised the Lord as we managed to get away, astonished at how quickly danger developed during our delightful day at the lake.

A similar event occurred at a crater at Mount Longonot. When we started out around the edge of the crater, it was a clear and lovely day, but as we progressed, a tiny cloud appeared. We were about halfway around the two-mile walk when a thunderhead formed, the temperature dropped, and the rain came down hard. Lightning struck above us as we laid down, just off the edge, crying out in our great danger. The storm passed, and God had delivered us once again.

More subdued vacations took us into the game parks, where we were overcome with thanksgiving for God's amazing humor in forming such a great variety of creatures. We simply reveled in the wonder of it all, especially enjoying the elephants and giraffes. Excursions in Kenya's game parks, and spending the night in huts, was especially daunting when I needed to assure local hunters that none of our daughters were available for a costly dowry.

It really was an extraordinary time. Our lives had taken remarkable turns, and we have been so grateful for God's direction.

From within the university and the fellowship center in East-leigh, from 1973 to 1979, I enjoyed six wonderful years studying and writing about the African worldview. Most of the books that I wrote were begun or dreamed about in Kenya—the entire culture was developing and Christianizing. I served on twenty-one committees at one time or another. It was a fruitful time.

Furthermore, the Mennonite bishop in Tanzania, Zedekiah Kisare, appointed me to direct the administration of the newly developing Kenya Mennonite Church. Joshua Okello joined me in pastoral ministries. For several years, this same bishop had authority for Mennonites in both Kenya and Tanzania, and he invited me to serve as pastor to the Nairobi church as well as the early beginnings of the church emerging in Mathare Valley nearby.

These were wonderful assignments for a university teacher and pastor—quite regularly, our children walked the two miles across town for Sunday church, and our family of six thrived. Grace and I were so thankful for our children's involvement in the life of the center and in the life of the emerging congregation.

Our home in Eastleigh on Eighth Street was viewed as a home of peace within the congestion of Eastleigh. And we were also located within a community of great diversity—our growing church served with other churches as an intertribal community committed to embracing the peace of Christ. We had Islamic, Christian, Buddhist, and Hindu neighbors, as well as a hundred different languages being spoken— absolutely phenomenal.

Where the gospel met these traditional cultures, there were lively engagements. One example was when an elder in the church decided to seek another wife because his first wife bore him only girls. After all, in his traditional religious view, it was children, not God, who gave him life after death. The traditional narrative we had come across in various parts of the African continent was clear—God had gone away, never to return, and this was a permanent, uncrossable divide. It seemed to me that this was why the birthing of children, and boys in particular, was so crucial. God may have forgotten us, but we could have children, and they would not forget.

But I wanted to communicate another way of thinking. So on Sunday I preached that Jesus, not our children, was our resurrection. It was in this way that we engaged the culture and introduced the gospel, bringing the peace of Jesus into the midst of our lives.

The transition from Somalia to Kenya was quite astonishing— in Somalia, after the Communist revolution, the rector of the university insisted that there was no space for God within the university; in Kenya, I was invited to teach religious studies within two weeks of our arrival. In Somalia, religious studies had become forbidden, while in Kenya, the constitution promised every student they could study the religion of their choice.

We loved our time in East Africa. In Kenya, I was employed to teach in the largest religious studies faculty in the world—my recollection is that the religious studies departments peaked at seven hundred students. The faculty in Nairobi was responsible for training high school teachers to teach faith studies in the high schools in Kenya. Muslim students could take a major in Islamic studies, and Christians could major in Christian theology.

I enjoyed my job teaching at the university in Kenya. Eighty percent of the schools in Kenya offered courses in Christian faith, and our faculty's job was to train the teachers who would be running those courses. A couple students I supervised worked on graduate studies, and they in turn became key leaders in Christian-Muslim relations.

Professorial regalia at Kenyatta University College, Nairobi, Kenya, where David served as a lecturer, 1975.

The Eastleigh Center was developing fruitfully as well as the Nairobi Mennonite Church. That center, with all of its diversity, was a sign of the reconciling presence of Jesus—these past number of years, the basketball teams go to tournaments throughout Nairobi and beyond, and the Eastleigh teams are known as the Menno Knights.

We felt grateful that we had these precious six years in Kenya. Looking back, I now remember that quite a few people advised us not to move to Eastleigh—in their minds, it was too dangerous. It was a rough area. They told us we wouldn't be safe there. Yet we felt safe from day one because the community took care of us.

On Sunday, either I or Joshua Okello preached, Grace played her accordian, and Ruth Mirenja, our dear friend, led the singing. We developed warm friendships, some of which have continued through the years. And I was able to do what many men do in Eastleigh: sit at a tea table on the sidewalk philosophizing.

Our children, along with their neighborhood friends, generated huge amounts of noise with barrels they retrieved from the construction site, challenging each other to jump from barrel to barrel.

Some months ago, Grace received a phone call from Canada. It was someone we had crossed paths with all those years ago, back at Eastleigh.

"Do you remember the cinnamon cookies you gave us when we played in your home, or the blue dress you gave me?" She went on to say, "I am now a refugee in Canada, and I met a pastor who led me to Jesus. I am sharing my newfound joy with many people."

In what many considered a dangerous area, this is what we were blessed to be part of.

12

Peacemaking among the Maasai

An important movement I became involved in was when the Maasai and other tribal groups asked the leaders of the Kenya Mennonite Church along with Eastern Mennonite Missions to help them become participants in Western Christianized culture, around 1977. They wanted to become Christians—the Maasai warriors had suffered losses in a battle, the kind of attack that was becoming more and more routine, and the clan elders agreed that the tribal conflicts were the result of a worldview problem that only Jesus could address. One of these problems was a metanarrative that said God originally bequeathed all of the cattle in the world to the Maasai, which led to many warriors believing that their responsibility was to get back all of the cattle that had gone missing from the Maasai. This led to endemic wars among the tribes, and often when I traveled into western Kenya I was disturbed by the fires that resulted from these conflicts.

Now the Maasai sought forgiveness and reconciliation.

I was appointed by the bishop of Tanzania to be an advisor, along with others, to participate in the transformation taking place. Kenyan Mennonite leaders were dynamically engaged from the beginning, and we found ourselves encouraging the Maasai in their rapid trek to meet Jesus Christ. I had never met their leaders before, although I knew some of the Luo tribal leaders of the Mennonite Church. Somehow, the Maasai had become convinced that Jesus was the key to effective peacemaking. So we sat down with their leaders and we began to work through their long-standing beliefs and practices that were keeping them from experiencing peace.

Maasai believers of Jesus who have laid aside their warrior traditions, from communities in both Ogwedhi-Sigawa and Oleopolis, Kenya.

A few days after one of my visits, thirty Maasai warriors were killed at the clinic on the Maasai, Kuria, and Luo border. The borderland village was known as Ogwedhi Sigawa meaning the border. The elders were appalled, and three different clans were involved, so all the elders were summoned. I was also invited, and we met right on the borderlands—this was before the Maasai became Christian, and during the same time that the Kuria were just beginning to consider Jesus as an option; the Luo were first and second generation Christians.

The spokesperson began by saying that for peace to happen in the region, all of the different clans needed to know that Jesus was the peacemaker, meaning all three tribes must worship together. Worshiping together meant being at peace with one another. In addition to worshiping together, all three clans needed to work together—this meant doing development work together. The elders wanted a cattle development project wherein the community could work together.

It was an important meeting, and it was the first step toward creating a lasting peace. From there, the elders formed a peacemaking committee and leaned heavily on the creation of pastors as significant roles in keeping that peace. A roster was created of all of the tribespeople committed to work for peacemaking—if a person would not submit to peace as upheld by the elders, that person was not welcome into the local store.

One example of this new commitment to peacemaking was witnessed when a Maasai warrior lost all of his cows to Kuria warriors in a nighttime raid. Normally, this kind of action would have resulted in bloodshed as the Maasai went to forcefully retrieve their cattle. But this time, Maasai peace warriors went straight to the Kuria pastor's home some distance away. The pastor went into the bush and found the stolen cattle, reminding the warriors that within their society there are stories of peacemakers. "Today," he told them, "let us conduct ourselves in ways that encourage peacemaking and let us lay aside our weapons."

That evening the warrior walked home with his cows, holding his Bible high so that all could see he was coming home in peace, carrying no weapons. It was a remarkable turn of events, one that went directly against the grain of their traditional response of retribution.

Do you see the power of the local church when it comes to peacemaking?

But even with a commitment to peacemaking, challenges arose. There was a lot of friction between newly-Christian Maasai and Luo who were mostly Christian as well, and this friction rose up around the treatment and respect of elders. Among the Luo, the elders in the church always went into a special room to eat Sunday dinner. Among the Maasai, in their traditional culture, everyone sat together as a congregation when having a festival.

Each side defended their practice with Scripture, but the tension was pulling the church apart, so the bishop convened an Acts 15 meeting—this is when the Jews and Gentiles in the early church convened over the sharp divisions being caused regarding the issue of circumcision for men. I was brought in as a consultant, and I sat beside the bishop, a few missionaries, and Luo pastors.

Eventually the congregation decided that the eating together issue would be a local matter, and each community would do what they thought was right. Elders could eat under the tree if they wished, or in the home, or with the congregation. The congregation's decision was clear and fair: local communities would be given freedom when it came to issues that didn't involve the Christian core beliefs.

They continued making decisions about other controversial topics—the Maasai unanimously decided to reject their warrior culture; they decided that having multiple wives was contrary to the gospel; drinking alcohol would be discouraged; the veneration of ancestors would cease.

After each question, the bishop would either say, "We have decided to lay aside this practice," or, "We have decided to encourage another practice." It was a revolutionary time, and I was honored to be part of the decision-making process.

On one occasion I was invited to participate in a reconciliation effort between Bishop Kisare in Tanzania and a pastor in Kenya. The issues were bringing deep strains between the Kenya and Tanzania Mennonite churches. We had a preliminary meeting at Shirati and the bishop said that a bishop approaching a pastor was not the way they do it in their traditional religions, but because of Jesus he would go so that they could become reconciled.

The meeting happened in a border village between Tanzania and Kenya over lunch. And it was going nowhere. The pastor presented a litany of grievances until finally the bishop got up, approached the pastor's chair, and leaned down, giving the pastor a hug.

"My dear pastor, can you forgive me for Jesus' sake so we can be reconciled?" he asked.

The pastor began to weep. He embraced the bishop and together we all sang the Hallelujah chorus of the revival as those two men embraced one another, weeping.

That reconciliation became a foundation for rebuilding the church between Kenya and Tanzania. As I worked at developing the Kenya Mennonite Church history years later (see chapter 15), I realized just how that entire history is marked with events bringing reconciliation again and again. That has been a deeply encouraging dimension of the life of the Kenya and Tanzania Mennonite churches. They decided to have two bishops ordained and the churches in Kenya thrived in the peace movement that the bishops were committed to.

As my university contract came to an end in Kenya, we had some decisions to make. Their policy was that guest professors could only have six-year terms, but the governing authority of the school passed a resolution saying they would make an exception in my case, asking me to extend my time there. I thanked them—it certainly meant a lot to me. But I felt awkward staying when the policy was so clear, and also there was a Kenyan wrapping up his PhD in the United States who I thought would be a perfect fit and should take my place.

The children were also ready to come home. Our oldest was eighteen years old, and we wanted to be with her as she settled into her new life in the United States. After careful consideration, Grace and I both felt it was time to leave Kenya. It was very hard to leave, and we could have easily continued there with great joy, but those around us who knew our family situation, knew what we had been through during our time in Somalia and Kenya, counseled us that it was time to step aside for a while.

The university said that if we weren't going to stay, they would at least have a going away party for me, so the graduating seniors and the faculty in the religious studies department threw a party. In a parting speech, the president of the university said he had a gift to give me, and he handed me a beautiful walking stick, dark wood, polished from top to bottom. There was a ring at the top, where you held the stick.

"This is a gift to you," he said in front of everyone. "I want to explain what it means. Notice that this hand carved in the stick is holding onto the ring at the top. This is something of great value. The ring represents the gospel that you have given witness to within the university setting. The whole university, from one end to the other, knows you are a follower of Jesus. That's what the ring is about—notice the hand carved into the stick holding the ring. That's you. Hang onto Jesus. If you hang onto Jesus, your life will continue being a blessing to all those around you. If you neglect this gift, you will become just a teacher. And you're a good teacher, but what has added to your teaching is your love for Jesus, and that is a blessing that has blessed our university. Farewell David Shenk. Hold onto the treasure that is Jesus."

He said this to the entire department. I had never really known where this man stood in relation to my confession of faith—he was a stereotypical broad-minded professor. But that day, after his speech, I knew in his heart of hearts he was right there with me, encouraging me to keep walking in the same way.

It was 1979, and we were returning to the States. I received an invitation to direct the Home Missions department at EMM as well as to pastor at Mountville Mennonite Church. We accepted both roles enthusiastically, and we looked forward to helping the children become involved in their new life in the United States . . . but I did wonder how we would all adjust after sixteen years in East Africa.

Part V

The World: God's Grace All the Way
(1980–2005)

13

Committed to the Center

It was 1980, and we were newly repatriated from Kenya. For both of us, but especially Grace, returning to the United States was a happy thing. She was glad to be home again, even though we had very little money, four children, and no place to live. One child would be heading off to college, the other three enrolled in Christian schools. But we were excited about the possibilities of serving God in Lancaster, and the invitation we had received from EMM to direct Home Missions was an excellent development.

We really had to count our pennies, but Grace's upbringing prepared her for that—she was, after all, a child of the Great Depression. And God opened doors, provided for us. A local farmer let us go and get milk from his milking parlor, and there were always opportunities for me to speak at churches.

Still, it was hard to ignore the numbers. I think we had managed to bring back $7,000 with us from Kenya, including money from our car fund, after all of those years of working abroad. During those years, interest rates were sky high and money was very difficult to borrow. We had no equity to speak of.

Shortly after getting home, I had an engagement in Hong Kong, which meant I needed to fly out immediately upon our return. Even with all of this on our minds, Grace and I decided to go out for ice cream so that we could connect before I left.

"Today while I was praying," she told me in the car. "I felt the Lord nudging us to go talk to your Uncle Tobias Leamen about loaning us money for a house."

Uncle Toby was the one who had provided carpentry equipment for my brother Joseph and me when we were boys in Tanzania. We used it in our shop in Mugango, and he had always been very interested in what we were up to.

It was 10:00 p.m. Instead of going by the ice cream shop, we agreed to drive by Uncle Tobias's house, and if there was even one light on, we would stop and have a word with him. Well, we drove to his farmhouse, and there it was—a light on in the bedroom. So we pulled up in front of the house, got out of the car, and went to the door.

I rang the bell, and Uncle Tobias answered the door in his bathrobe.

"David Shenk!" he exclaimed. "What are you doing?"

"Uncle Toby," I said. "We need a house, but we can't afford a mortgage at these interest rates. Would you loan us $20,000 at 10 percent interest?"

He didn't even hesitate.

"David and Grace, I'll have a $20,000 certificate to you tomorrow. I'd rather loan the money to my nephew than anyone else."

When people say there's no God, I think of "coincidences" like this one and think, *You have got to be kidding!* We lived in that house for forty years. The Lord just went ahead of us.

The other wonderful thing about our return was that EMM gave me an entire year to write, and I completed three of my books during that time. It was exciting, arriving home and being able to focus on writing. On top of that, I was traveling nearly every Sunday and preaching in Mennonite churches throughout Lancaster Mennonite Conference and beyond, often accompanied by Grace and the family. This was an enormous blessing.

I have to admit, though—in 1980, I was curious as to the environment I was returning to. Would issues over the strict Mennonite dress code weigh on us? Would they threaten to cause more fissures in our community?

Soon after I returned, my questions were answered.

When I became the pastor at Mountville Mennonite Church, I had no permission to wear a necktie in my district. I suppose five or ten men at the annual Lancaster Mennonite conference wore neckties—out of a gathering of three hundred pastors and leaders. Of course, I was still the bold pastor, so I asked our district bishop to open the door for me to wear a necktie in my ministry assignments. The reason I wanted to wear a necktie was because I wanted to identify with the culture and people whom I lived among. (Ironically, almost no one wears a necktie in my home church these days.)

He consulted other pastors in the area and agreed.

Eventually, I asked for one more favor.

"Could we have a meeting to decide whether the women in our congregation, if they wish, could be free to lay aside the head covering as well?"

The thought was so shocking that my bishop turned white. Perhaps I was moving too fast? Instead of pressing that issue, I asked if the congregation would endorse a six-month study on biblical interpretation. The bishop agreed to a time period of examining how to interpret the Bible, and in fact he led a few of those events. Eventually, we would have our Acts 15 meeting over these clothing issues, much as I had witnessed the Maasai having theirs not long before. It is in Acts 15 where the early church struggles through the decision of whether or not to require circumcision, a practice that many of them could not imagine doing away with. Our Lancaster Conference view of women wearing coverings was similarly ingrained in traditional Mennonite culture and scriptural understandings.

The day for the decision meeting arrived at Mountville, and we welcomed the entire congregation in on the conversation.

"We have learned," I said, "that every person in the church at Mountville is committed to the authority of the Bible—our differences arise out of our interpretations."

From there, we took action, encouraging everyone to continue wearing the covering especially for worship, but each woman was free to follow her own conscience. All women were free to wear or not to wear the covering, but we also encouraged everyone to submit to the authority of the Scriptures.

These kinds of fresh conversations freed congregations and individuals to hear the voice of the Holy Spirit and the teaching of Scripture. In fact, leadership conducted these conversations with such grace and humility that no one left our congregation at that time. There was no angry leaving of the church, no fractious split. The meetings injected a new level of freedom into the community, and our bishop supported us every step of the way.

It was an exhilarating time. We were on the cusp of transition taking place throughout the Mennonite church, from one end of the country to the other.

Another controversial conversation arose when a local man came to our patio to tell me that he could not be baptized because the men in his family always joined the military when our country was threatened, and he knew this was counter to the Mennonite way.

"Are you open to considering what we teach about the military, or do you reject that teaching in our church?" I asked him.

"Oh, no," he said, "I am open to what you are teaching. It's just that I am not yet persuaded." His openness to the teaching seemed the critical point to me—he was not disagreeing or refusing this part of Mennonite doctrine. He was still exploring it. So we agreed that he could be baptized as he continued his journey of exploring the meaning of peacemaking in the Bible.

This is what we mean when we talk about having a centered-set approach to beliefs and practices—we function without a fence, always praying that people would be drawn to the teaching at the center. The center is clear: Jesus. An open door with a clear center has always served our church well.

My views on peacemaking were greatly influenced by Heshbon Mwangi, a pastor in the Anglican church, whom I met in my adulthood. But this story really begins in 1948, when I was eleven years old and our family returned to East Africa after our home furlough, only to discover a very transformed community of nations rapidly emerging. Tanganyika was leaving its status as a United Nations territory. Kenya was plunging into civil war. Warriors were doing their best to collapse Kenya as a British colony. The war was called Mau Mau.

Fast forward to this time period, the early 1980s, and I was in Kenya riding my 80cc Honda cycle into the hills of the

central highlands. There I met Heshbon Mwangi, a pastor in
the Anglican church. We passed into the area where the Mau
Mau was especially a threat to the Christian congregations
and through the regions where a church commemorating the
martyrs was present. We stopped and sipped tea as I listened.

His face bore the deep scars of a machete where the warriors had attacked him, then left, thinking they had killed him.
The whole village ran. No one remained to rescue him.

I asked, "Why did you not take a gun and protect yourself?"

Heshbon's reply greatly influenced my thinking on peacemaking.

"In our traditional religions, if you drink the blood of the
sacrificial lamb, you can never do violence against the one who
has sacrificed for peace. If that is true of the ancestral blood,
how much more can you never do violence against those who
have been washed in the blood of the Lamb of God. How can
I kill anyone for whom Christ has died?"

The testimony of the church was that the wine and the
bread of the Christian communion service is the open hands of
Jesus calling all followers of Jesus into the covenant of peace
that is established by Jesus, the crucified Lamb.

During the Mau Mau many were martyred for their commitment to Jesus and his peace. Central to the *balokole* (revivalists—see Appendix I) peacemaking was Jesus the crucified
Lamb of God. When someone was martyred the balokole
would get a truck filled with singing balokole as they traveled
to the funeral praising God that another of their number were
counted worthy to die for Jesus. That witness, in time, contributed to the transformation of Kenyan society. The people
of the Lamb were a gentle witness that, in Jesus, forgiveness
and reconciliation brings healing and the miracle of the grace
of the cross.

Africans committed to the reconciling grace of Jesus were very significant in my embrace of both African and Anabaptist commitment to nonviolence and peacemaking.

All of these experiences informed my interactions.

When I arrived as pastor at Mountville in the early eighties, the congregation was down to thirty-five people on a Sunday morning—six couples then accepted the invitation to become a part of the congregation with a focus on mission. Our written confession of faith was not adequate, and several of us feared that without clearly stating it, we would fly apart.

In this way my work at EMM and my work at Mountville had similar goals—I wanted to increase our culture's understanding of the peace of Jesus and, as a result, grow our local churches. Because of this goal, much of my energy went into equipping church planters in the Anabaptist way.

We invited Ervin Stutzman to join the Home Ministry department, and he gave us leadership in developing a catechetical instruction, which was sorely needed. With a confession of faith and a new members' instruction, our pastors finally had tools that would help them become grounded in the faith. As a result, God prospered these commitments to love Jesus.

It was around this time that five of us missions directors met in Mountville with Myron and Esther Augsburger to consider releasing the Augsburgers to plant a church on Maryland Avenue on Capitol Hill in Washington, D.C. Myron was the former president of Eastern Mennonite University, and he was quite keen on the possibility of planting a church. We would be placing Anabaptists within the shadows of Washington, the center of worldly power. How could our center-set beliefs hold up under such scrutiny? Could a Mennonite church survive the inevitable pressure?

But first things first: could we even find an affordable building available on Capitol Hill?

As we developed our plan, we found a building, one that would cost us $150,000 to take over. We needed to raise the funds quickly, but we got down to the final week, and we were still $75,000 short. I wondered if perhaps this church in Washington, D.C., wouldn't happen. Then we got a phone call, at around 9:00 p.m. while we were staying in Harrisburg, Pennsylvania. The front desk called and said there was someone on the line for Dr. Augsburger.

When he picked up, the person introduced himself. "Last night my wife and I couldn't sleep—the Lord was impressing on us that we should contribute the remaining funds needed for your church building in Washington, D.C."

Myron danced a jig and, with tears of gratitude, we concluded the meeting praying our thanks. The next morning, we signed all the papers necessary to obtain the building.

We decided to move forward, and Myron and Esther did a trial run, choosing one Sunday morning to stand on the sidewalk outside of their building and invite passersby to come in and hear Myron preach. Seven people attended the first meeting of the Washington Community Fellowship. Eventually, four Home Ministry agencies joined hands to work with the Augsburgers in the development of what became a thriving community on Capitol Hill, attracting government, business, and political leaders. Myron even led a Bible study for military officers.

Planting this church in Washington, D.C., was a major shift from the typical way of doing church planting, at least for Mennonites. We were the quiet people in the land—at

Washington Community Fellowship, we were having Bible studies in the center of power.

On a personal note, it was enormously encouraging to work with Myron and Esther to acquire these facilities. The Capitol is the crossroads for millions of people every year, and the church became a dynamic congregation for representatives of the whole world who were in town on any given Sunday.

The reverberations significantly impacted the Mennonite denomination. In a period of rapid church growth there was a lot of uncertainty as to what kind of churches Mennonites should be planting. One stream of emerging churches had a rather Amish kind of theology; just be a presence. That is enough. Another stream was focused on evangelism and planting new churches all across North America. EMM was mostly very keen about planting churches. Others felt that these new churches will destroy the traditional Swiss-German communities from which Lancaster Mennonite Conference congregations had descended.

I'll never forget a meeting at the international students' hostel of the Allegheny Mennonite Conference. Myron Augsburger and Paul Peachey invested a morning debating what kind of churches Mennonites should plant. It was an intense meeting, and as we stood to leave, the issues were left unresolved.

Yet I'll never forget that at the end of that long conversation, the short Paul Peachey and the tall Myron Augsburger shook hands with one another.

"Today we have agreed," Paul Peachey said, "that you, Myron, and I, Paul, have an apostolate, and we will respect each other even though we disagree."

That conversation was an incarnation of the "presence" witness, or a "proclamation" witness, that converges within Mennonite church planting wherever we go.

We had used the catechetical instruction and confession of faith for our Mountville Mennonite community, and not long after that we sailed into turbulent waters regarding how to use the Mennonite Confession of Faith across Lancaster Mennonite Conference. The conference took these questions seriously—several of the leaders traveled to a number of our international partners to ask for their counsel on the direction we should take with our confessions. In fact, the American church returned to Kenya and Tanzania to receive counsel from the Maasai.

This is an Anabaptist commitment, this giving and receiving of counsel within the broader swath of the Mennonite movement. Imagine former Maasai warrior elders conferring with American Mennonites with Swiss German origins on what response Mennonites should have with respect to the Mennonite Confession of Faith! We were thrilled to live in a time when North American and East African Mennonites listened to one another with respect to matters of faith and practice. This interdependence is so important for the growth and flourishing of the church.

The international churches encouraged the American church to stand firm in its commitment to the new Mennonite Confession of Faith. This was verified later in Vietnam, where the *Confession of Faith in a Mennonite Perspective* was shared. The Vietnam churches EMM had partnered with found the confession so compelling that fifteen thousand people from the hill tribes took steps to become Mennonites! What an incredible movement. When they saw the Mennonite Confession of Faith, they realized that it was an accurate description of who they were and what they believed.

Those first years after we returned to the United States were full of these kinds of energizing and important conversations.

And they served as a foundation for what would begin to form next.

I served as director of EMM's international missions for ten years, engaging in conversations around the Mennonite Confession of Faith as well as Muslim and Christian peace-making. It was an invigorating time. Then, in 1997, just prior to Mennonite World Conference (MWC) in Calcutta, India, Richard Showalter and I invited persons and agencies who were in partnership with EMM to a three-day missions retreat for a get-acquainted fellowship. We met in Serampore, India, just prior to Mennonite World Conference. Seventy missions leaders convened from forty countries. The purpose of the gathering was to plan for a network of Anabaptist mission leaders from their respective countries, especially those who have been EMM partners.

Serampore was William Carey's home as he recruited missionaries from India and some from distant places. William Carey is the father of the modern missions movement. During this important time together, we told stories and prayed and planned. And out of that gathering we organized the first International Missions Association (IMA) meeting, to be held at the MWC in Calcutta. This was an opportunity for leaders in emerging churches that are in fellowship together to form an alliance of missions leaders who would partner with one another to commission and equip for worldwide missions. The planning committee decided that we would meet once a year.

It seemed to us that Thailand would be a good launching pad for the vision of IMA. I shared this with the Indonesian missions leaders of PIPKA (an Indonesian Mennonite church mission board) as well as with Richard Showalter, president of

EMM. They commissioned Andres Setiawan of PIPKA and me to find an unreached area in Thailand. I went in the capacity of director of the EMM International Missions program. We also contacted the Evangelical Council of Thailand, where we spent a whole day in prayer, spreading our maps out on the floor, and asking God to show the way. We investigated how many churches were in the area of each region, and our group agreed that our destination should be close to a train in case someone was stricken by illness in some remote place.

Skip and Carol Toban were helpful, for they knew the culture and the language well, and we decided to send the first IMA-related missionary to Det Udom in southeast Thailand. This was a significant event, the first step toward IMA placing international missionaries.

For us in the United States our first involvement with IMA was with Tibet. The interest came because of a young high school graduate from Reading, Pennsylvania, who in her prayers sensed the Holy Spirit saying that EMM should prepare for Tibet. That calling came to her as she was looking at a picture of Tibet in the National Geographic. That's when the Lord spoke to her.

Again, I am reminded of the gentle way in which Jesus calls us, the various ways in which He gets our attention and asks us to say yes. Fortunately, this girl moved forward in courage, sharing her vision from the Holy Spirit that we should prepare for ministry in Tibet, and we in turn began to explore what that might look like.

In due course, with cooperation between EMM and Indonesia, we were able to commission ministry to Tibet. This has been very fruitful in developing the theological foundations needed in establishing a church within Buddhist Tibet.

Of course, taking Christianity into a new and different culture always comes with its fair share of challenges and opportunities. Very early on in Thailand the EMM team and the IMA experienced a surprising conflict swirling around the issue of Buddhist strings. The missionary team encountered deeply felt convictions around the question as to whether or not symbols of Buddhism could continue in the life of a new Christian. The strings were the ultimate symbol of identification for a Buddhist, akin to baptism in the Christian faith. Buddhists received these identification strings in certain stages of growing up. The team struggled with those who believed that it was possible to transform Buddhist strings into the symbols of Christian church or whether they should be excluded. The word and concept that they struggled with was *contextualization*.

As I left Thailand, I went on to Singapore and was able to attend a Sunday morning service at a Methodist church. The bishop preached on the theme, "We cannot serve two masters," reading from Matthew 6:24.

> No one can serve two masters. Either you will hate the one and love the other, or you will be devoted to the one and despise the other. You cannot serve both God and money.

The message of that sermon should not be taken lightly. We encouraged the Christians in Thailand to keep this in mind as they made decisions regarding which parts of their Buddhist heritage could be retained and what needed to be left behind.

From Calcutta until today that sense of calling for unreached peoples has persisted within this partnering Anabaptist group of churches which formed the first IMA meeting in Serempore. The IMA is fulfilling a need for mission vision that carries us beyond storytelling to planning to actually support missionaries like we have done in Thailand.

Several years after the IMA was formed, a gathering in Mexico felt that we needed to invest more time in prayer and seeking the fullness of the Spirit as we engaged missionaries in frontiers where the gospel has never been known. This led us to focus on four dimensions during our annual meeting:

- The IMA gathering reporting on what has been happening in missions within the respective churches that participate.
- A one-day Holy Spirit conference for prayer, fasting, and discernment with a commitment to welcoming the Holy Spirit in his ministries of empowerment and discernment.
- A field trip to become personally involved in mission within the community or region where we are meeting.
- Inviting laborers into the harvest field while providing seminars to become fruitful witnesses of the gospel.

Most importantly, the door is always open for others to join the IMA movement. The emergence of IMA gives me much joy as emerging churches joined together to partner for the global movement of the gospel. May God be praised!

14

Off to LCC International University

During the decade of the 1990s I felt a growing conviction that I should plan more time for writing and leadership formation. We had learned so much during the previous thirty years, so many things that I wanted to communicate not only to the Mennonite community but to the world, to people of all races and religions. Especially, I felt an intense desire to share about the peace of Jesus to a wide audience.

Grace and I shared with the Lord that when a door opened for a ministry that allowed for more equipping, we would be quite ready to walk through that door. We had spent an incredible nineteen years of administration with Eastern Mennonite Missions, but it became clear that the time was at hand to move forward into something new. We had served together in New York City, Somalia, Kenya, and now as missions directors in the United States—we were both rather excited to see what might come next.

I had become acquainted with LCC International University in Klaipėda, Lithuania, because Eastern Mennonite Missions was providing a couple of teachers for the university. I was very excited about the mission of LCC—one common thread in my life, ever since I was a boy in Tanzania and my parents were setting up local schools, was involvement in creating systems of education for communities where this did not exist. Little did Grace and I know that our next call would be very much along these lines.

I was delighted when I was traveling through Lithuania and had lunch with Professor Jim Mininger, the president of LCC. As we spoke, he invited me to join the team as academic dean and for Grace to serve as student counselor. I felt my spirits soar—this was it! This was the next call, the challenge I had been waiting for.

But what would Grace think? Would she be ready to return to overseas missions after nineteen years in the United States?

I hopped on the plane home, and I called Grace as soon as the plane landed, telling her about the opportunity awaiting us in Lithuania.

She wept.

There had been challenges in getting the family settled when we returned from Kenya nearly twenty years before, and Grace had always felt that one of her primary calls was to be a mother to our children. Now, the door was opening to be a grandmother, so she wasn't eager to go overseas again. And none of the children wanted us to go, either. They had been hoping we could be there for them during their later years.

David and Grace at Lithuania Christian College, where David was academic dean and Grace student counselor, 2001.

Lithuania Christian College, with graduates Saulius and Sanna, a pastoral couple in Lithuania, 2004.

It took Grace a few months to work through this question. But we continued processing it with our pastor and our prayer team. One night, our pastor looked at Grace and said, "Grace, it is time to go. How do you feel?"

Grace said, through tears, "Yes. It's time to go."

Fortunately, the contract with LCC would allow us to get home at times to be with our family. And Grace would have a specific role that would allow her to use her recently earned degree in pastoral counseling.

"Now I know why I felt such an urgency to get that degree," Grace said as we prepared to leave.

Even then, Grace still sought a sign from God that she was doing the right thing. As we flew into Lithuania, Grace told God, *If there is a plant in our new home, if I walk in and see a houseplant, that would be the sign I need to confirm this.*

We walked up the five flights of stairs, unlocked the door, and right there in front of us was a huge houseplant.

Thank you, Lord.

Grace threw herself into ministry in Lithuania.

"If I had a nice set of dishes for guests, it would make me feel at home."

We purchased the dishes and proceeded to host people at our home almost every Friday night. One of the first matters we attended to was to get acquainted with the pastors in town. We brought with us a letter of recommendation from Mountville Mennonite Church and asked to become members accountable to the church and the pastor. If we missed a Sunday, we got in touch with the pastor and let him know where we were. We built trust and formed a pastors' fellowship, participating joyfully in the life of the church even though our foreign language abilities were limited.

Within several months of arriving in Lithuania I needed to take Grace to Vilnius for a flight to the States for a medical situation. That is a three-hour trip from Klaipėda where we lived, during the post-Soviet era when gasoline systems were as yet very rare. In addition to the inconvenience of trying to find gasoline along the route, the weather was bitterly cold. I was a new arrival and still unaware that one could not purchase gasoline for long stretches. Such was my naivete.

During my return trip to our home in Klaipėda, I ran out of gasoline with fifty kilometers to go. I have to admit—I was terrified. Nighttime traffic does not stop along the expressway, and I knew I would freeze to death without intervention. I prayed that God would miraculously save me from this catastrophe.

After waiting as long as I could, I decided the only way forward was to walk those fifty kilometers in ten-degree weather. If I sat in my car, I would freeze—at least if I was walking, I had a chance to make it to morning. And maybe some Good Samaritan would stop and help if they saw me walking along the highway.

As I set off, I noticed a car had stopped across from me on the expressway. As I neared the car, I noticed there was a woman vomiting in the snow, and a man sitting next to her in the car.

I asked them what was wrong—they were surprised to see me walking through the snow. She had lost her purse in Vilnius, and with it her passport and other important papers. She was sick with anxiety. They needed to return to Vilnius and would drop me off at a gas station up the road, promising to pick me up on the way back, returning me to my car with gasoline.

So they did. I got into the car with them, they dropped me off at the gas station, and then headed on their way to find her purse. When they finally picked me up on the return trip, the woman said, "The Lord answered both our prayers, mine for my purse and yours for gasoline."

We returned to my vehicle, and even though it was a diesel, it started immediately. But the next morning, when I was back at home, our diesel car would not start because of the cold. I still think about how amazing it was that their car stopped exactly across the expressway from where I was standing and that they had not seen me. I thanked God again for commissioning angels to care for me.

Lithuania Christian College, now LCC International University, was developed by invitation of Lithuanians within the government who believed that a Christian university was necessary to provide leaders who have been formed by Christian values. Those values, as they recognized them, were first, an entrepreneurial spirit, second, a respect for the other person, and finally, integrity. Most of the potential students who would attend the college were not Christians, but they were reaching for values that could equip them in a postcommunist society.

One of my students, during a short walk from the dormitory to the classrooms, told me, "Dr. Shenk, I hope you are taking this class seriously because we are! This is the first exposure we have had to the Christian faith, and we are making decisions about the values that will guide our lives."

I thought on his words often.

As we learned together, they came to realize that these values were derived directly from Genesis 1: God created Adam and Eve in his own image. The world of science, while it can bring wonderful breakthroughs in medicine and health (as we experienced during my childhood in Tanzania), has limitations. It cannot deliver these beautiful truths having to do with our identity and meaning—these can only be derived through revelation. Science cannot tell us why we are here on planet Earth.

This assertion, that humans were created in the image of God, stirred vigorous discussion and debate in my theology classes. The foundational question we had to explore was: *Am I just a monkey, or am I created in God's image?* To say we were created in God's image is a huge transformation, especially among societies where there often seems to be apathy, or even disdain, for human life.

The belief that every human being has been created in God's image affects every area of our lives. This was a belief preserved by the grandparents in Lithuanian society during the long, deep night when Marxist philosophers attacked people of faith. Students in my class frequently said their grandmother whispered in their ear from time to time, "You are a Christian, for I arranged for you to be baptized secretly during the time when Marxism prevailed." Some would tell me, "I have decided to follow the faith of my grandma."

In my classes at LCC, we committed ourselves to the three values listed above: an entrepreneurial spirit, respect, and integrity. Occasionally a student would write me a note saying, "Last night I made the U-turn," and I would shed some tears of joy, for I knew those words meant that they had made a choice to follow Christ.

Another special joy we were able to experience in Lithuania was inviting each of our four children with their families to visit us. This was a new part of the world for us and those visits were wonderful, as we were able to explore with our children and grandchildren.

Academically, our time in Lithuania invigorated and inspired me. A couple of my books were translated into Lithuanian, including *Surprises of the Christian Way*, which was translated by a few of my students. They said, "Our parents don't know what the Christian approach in the college is about." That book became my textbook in the course on theology.

Our time in LCC was equally rich for Grace, who had received a specific call to be a counselor there for the students. Most of her time was spent in Bible studies, teaching new Christians about the peace of Jesus. We had been obedient in following the call yet again, and God proved faithful to us during our time there. It was another time of rigorous conversations, where Grace and I engaged secular culture and learned more about the questions of our time. We learned more about what contemporary culture was looking for, namely the search for meaning and values. And, most importantly, these years gave us the opportunity to bear witness to the work of God in the world.

What a gift.

After four years we concluded our assignment by travelling for LCC. The university asked us to invest the fall in traveling in Europe and Central Asia, recruiting students for the university. That put us on the road for sixteen weeks, and during that time we visited twenty countries. We will never forget that life-changing travel, but what stands out is our first week on the road.

We arrived at the border between Lithuania and Belarus at noon to begin our journey. Traffic on the Belarusian side was backed up as the officers needed a drink that took most of the afternoon. Consequently, it was dark when we got into Belarus, and we had been warned not to drive into Belarus after dark. We were frightened.

We were wondering what to do when two English-speaking expatriates in front of us at the border graciously gave us their map of Belarus, which was in Russian, and instructed us on how to read it. I tried to bring to memory my biblical Greek, as the Belarusian alphabet has similarities to modern-day Greek, and we headed off for Brest, Belarus. Of course, we had no GPS and the mobile phone was only recently available in Belarus. It was only after we left that we discovered there were no hotels along the way, and we found ourselves in this large city at midnight not knowing the language and not knowing exactly where we were. We finally arrived at 2:00 a.m. in what we hoped was the correct church parking lot. We phoned Olga, a student at LCC. She answered! We thanked God for providing angels to protect us.

That was the launch pad for a fabulous four months on the road.

I spoke three times the next day in atheistic Belarus about Christian university education. I could tell that my message was astonishing to them—the assumption in the university world at that time and place was that the Christian faith was uninformed and false. But when people heard the message I was delivering, along with the societal and cultural benefits of Christian colleges, interest in LCC increased. Within several years enrollment at the college had reached 650 students, some of whom became believers in Christ. So many positive relationships were formed along the way.

In one city, as we met with the high school principal to try to arrange for us to tell her students about LCC, she said, "We don't want religion here. It frightens us."

I replied, "We are also afraid of religion, but we are committed to Jesus, not religion. Jesus says we are created in his image and therefore we should love one another." She immediately rang the bell and called all students and faculty for an assembly to hear about Jesus and about LCC.

The amount of interest we received in the college was astonishing, but it shouldn't have been surprising—it was an American-style, Christian liberal arts college education for only $2,000 a year. The students came to LCC because there was something about the Christian ethos that nurtured respect for the person, and at LCC, no matter who you were or where you came from, you were respected. The appreciation for critical thinking and an entrepreneurial spirit also attracted students from far and wide.

At the end of our twenty-week marathon we arrived back to LCC to report on our trip, then home to the United States for Christmas. What I didn't realize at the time was that my engagement with Muslims would soon become our central area of ministry.

Back when we had been preparing to leave for our four-year assignment in Lithuania, I received a handwritten note from Canada inviting me to engage with Muslims in a gentle encounter. A follow-up letter came from the United Kingdom, and at the time I assumed it was from a student Christian group. It took me several months to understand the nature of the invitation.

The first session was to take place at the large central Islamic center in the heart of London, with a three-hour engagement on the topic of revelation. The event was being sponsored not by a Christian group like I had thought, but by the Muslim Student Association for the United Kingdom. I was able to accept that invitation because the meeting would take place during a January school break while I was at LCC International University.

The plan was to facilitate six engagements, three hours each, on six consecutive nights. When I arrived at the mosque on a Saturday evening, it was exhilarating. I couldn't wait to see how the engagement would go. But when I walked into the building, I was astounded by what I saw in front of me: five hundred Muslims packed wall to wall, most leaning forward to be sure they missed nothing. I was very grateful for the half dozen representatives from the small London Mennonite communities, but besides them, it was an overwhelmingly Muslim event.

Often, when inviting me to speak, people would say, "We have invited you because you love Muslims and you love Jesus." I cannot in words express how overwhelming and how important it seemed to me, that Muslims would sense my love for them, so as I stood there, I prayed for holy boldness. I went into the auditorium praying that I would speak with clarity and with gentleness and truthfulness, exalting Jesus.

The Muslims chose the themes: the crucifixion, the Trinity, the Scriptures, the cross, salvation, and the Son of God. The dialogue was very well-organized. It soon became evident that some of the students intended to counter my commitment to Christ. Their questions sometimes went beyond probing and bordered on aggressive, questioning the integrity of my faith or the veracity of the Christian worldview in an attacking way. Repeatedly I said to my Muslim host that in Lithuania where I am a professor, I expect atheists to attack my faith—that never surprises me.

"I am astonished that a number of you Muslims, who are commanded in the Qur'an to respect the Christians and their Scriptures, and are believers in God and in all the scriptures, are attacking the very scriptures that the Qur'an says you should believe in."

This got their attention and we all thought twice about how we were interacting.

"I am called to give witness to the Scriptures that God has entrusted to me but I will not attack your scriptures," I said.

During the event, I was allowed to distribute books, and I even included the address of the London Mennonite Center in the books. Some of the students at the event later asked for addresses so they could connect with Christian students in a kind of letter exchange.

Others even spoke of following Christ. "We want to become Christian but we don't know anyone here in the university who believes what you are saying."

I knew that most of these students had never heard an exposition of the Christian faith.

During one exchange my Muslim companion spoke disrespectfully of redemption, so I walked across the platform to where he was standing and embraced him. He was rather confused! But I said, "Redemption is God seeking to find you and embrace you. Do not disrespect such great love."

I have never in my life spoken to such an intensely interested audience, and I am deeply grateful that what happened in London was the first of other opportunities for dialogues as well. It was remarkable. I am thankful for that door that God opened. The events were filmed, and those six videos were subsequently published and circulated widely. During these many years in which I have engaged with Muslims, most of them seem to have seen those videos. I have often prayed that God would take those videos and speak even though I was inadequate to such a challenge; however, I believe the participants did see Jesus.

15

Let God Surprise You

When we completed our tenure with LCC International University and returned to the United States in 2002, Grace and I thought we were simply coming back to the States, but doorways began opening in the academic world that allowed us to be very fruitful. Richard Showalter, who was the EMM president, invited me to become his global consultant for EMM with special focus on Islamic ministries and peacemaking. We of course assured him that we would be honored and grateful for that kind of appointment, but we would need a team to work with us. This is why we had an oversight committee of twelve members who met with us periodically for counsel, prayer, and accountability.

Almost immediately after taking this post, I began receiving invitations from around the world to serve as a consultant for peacemaking. Sometimes I wore the academic hat of LCC and at other times I wore the consultant's hat, accountable

Serving
Globally

**Grace and David
Shenk**

Christian/Muslim relations
consultants

Home congregation:
Mountville Mennonite Church
Mountville, PA

Eastern Mennonite Missions

EMM

Going where the church is not ... yet.

Do not post this information on any websites

Prayer card for distribution to supporters and churches while serving as global
consultants with EMM, 2002.

to Richard Showalter at EMM. Being in that position, and
having the history and experience that I had, introduced me to
some surprising possibilities.

These opportunities in the world of academia and missiology allowed me to have influence in unique areas.

It was August 2003, at Mennonite World Conference in
Zimbabwe, that Bishop Oponde stepped out of the lunch line
and pulled me aside.

"David," he said, "the Kenya Mennonite Church has chosen you to write a history of the Kenya Mennonite Church. It
must be done now because the early pioneers are going to their
heavenly reward. We are asking you to carry this responsibility."

I had not heard of the project before, but the thought of
being involved in something so special moved me. "I cannot
write that book myself," I said. "There must be two people
working on it together, and the Kenyan should be Francis
Ojwang'. Then we need a team for counsel as we go along."

I was so excited. We shook hands with a promise to do what we could.

A year later when I was in Migori, Francis Ojwang' and I met with several Mennonite church leaders to make our plan to write that book. It was an eight-year project, a miracle project. We were blessed when Laura Kurtz, a retired missionary from Tanzania, consented to work with us, and so the three of us began organizing and writing this amazing book.

A committee was appointed, and we met together occasionally. Francis carried us forward by going into every village where there was a Kenya Mennonite church. He would sit there with his computer, and he conducted interviews in every region of the Kenya Mennonite Church. What an enormous commitment! We worked with different language groups, sometimes with illiterate people.

Then we had to organize the narrative. We had to ask questions like: Which section comes first? Which comes last? Who should be included? What will we do if there is criticism? We decided to write the book like the book of Acts, where both

Enjoying tea in the home of Francis and Eveline Ojwang', in 2016, on a family visit.

the good and the not so good are reported and the grace of our Lord Jesus Christ is exalted.

The book reinforced that we are all saved by grace, for so many of us in this book reveal characteristics that we might wish were different. For example, in one chapter there was critique of my leadership. I didn't like to read that, but I believe it is true. As I have grown older, I've come to better understand my own personal weaknesses, and that makes it easier to accept correction. I am a sinner saved by grace.

Finally, the day came to test the manuscript. The total writing team was eleven people. We met in Nairobi, and a representative from every region of Kenya came together. Sentence by sentence we read through the book, always asking the question: Is what we say true? Is it kind? Does it celebrate God's grace in Christ?

It was that simple.

The writing team, led by Francis Ojwang' with David serving as associate editor and Laura Kurtz as assistant, for *Forward in Faith: History of the Kenya Mennonite Church*, 2004.

After the reading of the sentences chapter by chapter we held discussions on the content, and in this way everyone was able to speak their opinions on the content and the manuscript was finalized. We called the book *Forward in Faith: History of the Kenya Mennonite Church*. The dhow, to represent the first missionaries who came in a fishing boat, is pictured on the front cover.

One dimension of the book that surprised me was including so many of the children's names. When I asked him about this, Francis would always respond by saying, "The children in the village where church is beginning must be named, for years from now some high school student will pull this book from his shelf in his living room. His face will glow as he says, 'That's my name. I am included in the book. Grandmother also was here for the first gathering of believers.'"

Church leaders invited our daughter Karen to Kisumu for the launching of the Kenya Mennonite Church history book. This was a significant event, with church leaders participating from Kenya and Tanzania, all of us celebrating together the wonderful story of the peace of Jesus moving through Kenya.

The Mennonite church leadership in Tanzania went through some rocky water, in some ways similar to Mennonites in North America during the last twenty years. We had gone through a challenging time, and then decisions were made that called for some positive changes. Don Jacobs, Noah Hershey, and I were invited to come celebrate as the local church leadership brought healing through the ordination of two bishops in Dar es Salaam. The church longed for a time of civility and joy to celebrate God calling forth new leadership in Tanzania, and we wanted to bring as many people together as possible for the ordination service, hoping to continue the process of healing and renewal taking place.

We passed the hat to raise money to get tickets for everybody in leadership roles in the Tanzania or Kenya Mennonite Church to attend. They rented a full railroad car with some of the seating space on grain sacks on the floor. The train left from Mwanza, Tanzania, for a forty-eight-hour trip, two wonderful days together in this reserved car. They had testimony meetings and song fests as they went through villages and towns. There was a kind of exuberance, integrity, love, and joy that we experienced in that wonderful train ride.

Finally, the next morning, we arrived in Dar es Salaam just in time for the ordination, and we found our way to the locale for these ordinations accompanied by traffic police and motorcycles. That was an ordination that I am sure filled heaven with joy—it wasn't a service made up only of formalities, but a time for all of us to recall the long journey of the church in Tanzania and all that had transpired to bring us to that special day.

Some of the stories of the Mennonite Church as a reconciling community were remarkable. On one occasion for nearly two months a pastor kept under his bed a man from another tribe who was being chased by his enemies. Protecting the enemies became a mission of the Mennonite Church in Kenya, as was providing food in times of interclan conflict, with assistance by Mennonite Central Committee.

Over the years the Kenya and Tanzania Mennonite Churches have taken seriously their commitment to cherish a peace-making legacy.

During these busy years of international travel, in 2005, I was en route to Nyabange, Tanzania, at the request of my brother

Joseph to speak at the Bible college for a week, and I received terrible news. My brother Joseph had died.

He liked to jog in the early morning, as did I, and he had been out at 6:00 a.m. for his daily run when a charcoal truck came down the one-mile hill above the college, lost control, and toppled over, crushing him. He was in the hospital for a short time with a damaged aorta that went undetected—it was this condition that killed him.

His death was an awful blow. He was very involved in the Bible college, the acting principal at the time, and he and I had so much been looking forward to spending time together. I thought of us as being quite the team through the years, whether it was as teenagers building furniture or running our trapping company, or later in life, working in East Africa. Our relationship as brothers was genuine and deep, and we had a way of counseling each other that we rarely received from anyone else.

I thought of him and my mother, Alta, and all the many other friends and family who have died during these years. At the same time that Joseph died, his son-in-law Reuben Stoltz-fus died in a car accident in Harrisonburg, Virginia. This was a time of deep grief. It is painful to lose those we love. But time and time again I am reminded of God's love for them, for me, and I take comfort that even after they are gone, Jesus remains.

Part VI

Christians and Muslims Engaging for Peace in Their Respective Ways (2005-2020)

16

Dynamic Engagement with the House of Islam

Throughout the years of our service, Grace and I have been involved in Christian-Muslim relations. This calling to bear witness to the peace of Jesus in a Muslim context has been affirmed again and again. This was the work we were being called to, and we both engaged in it with enthusiasm. Muslims and Christians both desire peace, for themselves as well as for their communities and nations. This longing for peace is a universal, human condition.

Some might point to violence in the Middle East as evidence to the contrary, but the many conversations we have had with Muslims around the world only serve to confirm their desire for peace. The following are various places around the world where Muslim authorities have invited Grace and me to enter into conversations promoting peace.

MOLDOVA

While the Soviet Union was collapsing, visionaries in Lithuania were imagining a post-Soviet society. The same vision was sweeping through Moldova, which had a significant evangelical and orthodox community. Grace and I were invited to Moldova to equip students to profess Christ within the secular-Muslim culture of Central Asia.

This sounded exciting to us, but our experience getting to Moldova was not pleasant. When we arrived in Ukraine for transit to Moldova, officials arrested us in the airport, where we spent two miserable, cigarette smoke–filled nights in the lounge. They also threatened us with deportation back to New York and a $15,000 fine. At one point we heard the announcement asking people to board the plane to New York, and we were even ushered to the jetway to board the New York plane, but we refused to go in and walked to the opposite side of the lounge. Immigration rejected our entry visa as invalid—the immigration officials were following the law, and in the Russian visa we had asked for multiple entries but had received a single-entry stamp. After a day and a half of uncertainty and discomfort, a senior official came to us in the lounge apologizing, gave us food, and sent us on our way to Moldova. I suppose they realized we weren't going to leave anytime soon.

When we arrived in Moldova late at night a sympathetic customs officer opened the doors for our entry. We were introduced to several faculty at the college and that was the beginning of a ten-year engagement with the Baptist Riches of Grace Theological University, whose name in Moldova is

Divitia Gratiae University. From that point we were asked to teach for two weeks every year at the university. Most of the students had Muslim backgrounds and had grown up among Soviet secularists. When the Soviet system collapsed, Baptists committed themselves to forming a bilingual and bicultural track in their emerging Christian university—the goal became having the graduates of the university return to their home areas and become pastors, founders of institutes, and directors of business enterprises.

Many of these students were Gagauz Turkic in ethnicity. Their traditional faith is Orthodox and they mostly live in Moldova. When a church commissions a Gagauz to go and minister among Turkic people in Central Asia, the local people say, "How can you be a Christian and Turk—aren't all Turks Muslim?" The Gagauz, although Turkic, were never Muslim.

God has equipped the Gagauz for ministry within Turkic societies. The college has Moldovan, Gagauz, Romanian and Central Asian students, and together they make a strong crosscultural community. And that was our assignment for ten years, meeting and teaching in the classroom. I mostly taught two classes there: "The Essence of the Christian Faith in a Muslim Context," and "Practical Engagement with Muslims."

There is a Christ-ward movement among the Turkic people, many of whom are coming to faith in Christ. In this kind of engagement you just marvel how the Lord put it together for doors opening among the Turkic people. The whole of Turkic culture is in various ways influenced by this university.

Moldova is the crossroads of Central Europe and Central Asia. Both continents meet in Moldova, and the cultures of the regions converge there. As you might imagine, the singing in the chapel is wonderful, and sometimes the space is filled with up to four languages worshiping together.

A dinner with Victor Ormanji, director of Central Asian ministries at Riches of Grace University, Moldova, along with his wife Julia and family in their home.

Perhaps the most miraculous element is that in this college Asia and Europe meet and share their faith with one another as well as testimonies of the Holy Spirit moving in their communities. In my classes every student is invited to share their story of meeting Jesus. Those stories are amazing. Truly the Holy Spirit is at work in communities all around the world.

KOSOVO

For years we prayed for Kosovo as well as Albania because there were no Albanian churches. With the collapse of communism we rejoiced that the door for sharing the good news in Kosovo was opening, and for that reason, I began visiting Kosovo as often as I could.

In 2015, I suggested to our EMM appointee in Kosovo that we explore the possibility of public dialogue between Christians and Muslims and explained why I thought our book, *A*

Muslim and a Christian in Dialogue, could be a tool to help facilitate that. But when we visited the academic Islamic faculty in Pristina, they made clear that they had no interest in dialogue with evangelicals about faith in Kosovo.

"We have just had a war," was the response. "We don't want more conflict."

So we gave them a few copies of the book and said, "If you have a change of mind let us know. We are in town for a couple days."

The next day we received a phone call and one of the professors said he had changed his mind.

"If this dialogue between Shenk and Kateregga leads to peacemaking, not to violence, then yes, we would like to have a dialogue with Shenk while he is in town."

So the hour and the day was set and announcements sent out everywhere.

On the evening when the dialogue was to happen, I sat beside the theologian who would be my counterpart.

"Shenk," he said, "every Christian and Muslim leader in Kosovo is here tonight. What we are seeing, with these hundreds of people coming into this great hall? We have never experienced anything like this."

The interest was electrifying. For two and a half hours we conversed with one another about the nature of peace in Islam and the nature of peace in the gospel. It was with profound gratitude that we headed home.

The next year our EMM appointee in Kosovo met me at the airport with some exciting news.

"The director of the Islamic faculty is asking that we come for round two, in order to discuss the themes of truth and freedom. We will close the university so that all students and faculty can come to hear how faith affects truth and freedom."

It was quite daunting, finding enough space: the university was packed out. I spoke on Genesis 1, specifically how we were created in God's image, and how Adam and Eve were equally created in God's image. And then I shared witness to the meaning of the cross as the place where we see the full revelation of God's love for us. After the lecture, there was time for questions. Again, the talk was very well received by Christians and Muslims alike.

I was told that my lecture was debated for the next three weeks. I knew that the reason they wanted me to speak was because Kosovo was struggling with its developing constitution. Should Kosovo become an Islamic state or a secular state with religious freedom for all? I suggested they lean upon the Bible, the first book of revelation that all Muslims and all Christians believe to be revealed Scripture. What would their constitution look like if that were a foundational commitment, if they treated people with the understanding that they were created in God's image?

A representative of the constitution committee took the pastor of the Protestant Evangelical church out to dinner after that lecture, and they decided to work together to support a constitution that would respect freedoms for both Christians and Muslims. When the constitution was finally drafted in Kosovo, it included an article that guaranteed freedom of religious choice.

These experiences prove to me that people have a deep longing for peace all around the world.

CHICAGO

Over the years, our EMM Christian-Muslim Relations Team has developed a relationship with Dr. Sayyid Syeed, now the former director of the Islamic Society of North America

(ISNA). Out of that friendship, we received a request to give out three thousand copies of *A Muslim and a Christian in Dialogue* for distribution at the ISNA convention in 2017, held in Chicago, Illinois. Special offerings and donations made it possible for us to fulfill that request.

The invitation was in harmony with what we're trying to create: Muslims and Christians coming together for respectful, civil conversations. In the main session, Dr. Sayyid encouraged everyone to be sure to take a copy of the book, and it led to many fruitful conversations and an ongoing spirit of goodwill that we have maintained to this day. Many participants were eager for the *Dialogue* because it helped them to understand their Muslim or Christian neighbor. Our Muslim host estimated that there were six thousand participants; as far as we know Grace and I, along with Andres and Angelica, our teammates, were the only Christian participants at this convention.

Muslims tend to like *A Muslim and a Christian in Dialogue* because they feel Islam is well-represented and Christians like it because they feel Christianity is also fairly presented. The purpose of the book is to cultivate understanding, a limited but important dimension in building relationships. The book has been translated into thirteen languages and used by Muslims and Christians to open the door to congenial conversations between Muslims and Christians.

One of my favorite stories from that convention was when a Muslim attendee told me that their twelve-year-old son picked up the book and read it long into the night. To think that what we wrote was understandable by a young person showed me that we had written it with the correct level of simplicity.

Of course, there was also the moment when a sincere follower of Islam tried to convert Grace by quoting numerous

David and Grace ready for another journey.

David with Dr. Sayyid Syeed and Andres Prins, discussing distribution of nearly 3,000 copies of the *Dialogue* at the annual gathering of the Islamic Society of North America, 2017.

biblical proof texts that appeared contradictory. Grace assured the person that her faith was satisfied.

These were the kinds of intense and meaningful conversations we wanted to engage in.

UGANDA

The book *A Muslim and a Christian in Dialogue* has made a similar impact in other places as well. Badru Kateregga, co-writer of that book, invited me to come to Uganda and join him in a series of seminars held at the university he had established, Kampala University. This was in 2018, shortly after the fortieth anniversary of the publication of *A Muslim and a Christian in Dialogue*. Our son Jonathan, a businessman, was invited to write and present a paper on spiritual foundations for enduring business principles, and Peter Sensenig was invited to present a paper on refugees. The presentations of these two young men were well received. And the dialogue events on peacemaking were acclaimed.

We planned a lively, one-week forum on Islam and the gospel where we would discuss the approach of Islam and the gospel in regard to transforming and creating society. The evening of our opening session I was astounded to be led into the assembly hall filled with four hundred professors and students. Kateregga orchestrated all of this and presented a fervent paper on the absolute necessity for civil society to flourish.

"Dialogue is the means for learning tolerance," declared Kateregga.

In all of this, my friend Kateregga was the perfect host. Kateregga heard that my son Jonathan was a Presbyterian minister, so Kateregga sent people to investigate how Presbyterians worship, and he had a Presbyterian clergy member come and lead us in a mixed Muslim and Christian environment in the way Presbyterians do.

Kateregga and his team also built a grass-thatched worship center for this event, and they asked me to preach a short sermon.

"As a boy living inland from the shores of Lake Victoria," I explained during my presentation, "one evening the man from Galilee met me, and ever since that day I have been his follower."

I asked whether dialogue alone is adequate to reveal all dimensions of truth, and Kateregga responded, "In a civil society both dialogue and belief belong together for it is in dialogue that we respect diversity. It is in belief that we discover one another as embracing faith that creates solid friendships such as David and I are experiencing tonight."

A Mennonite bishop also preached, and then an imam spoke. Kateregga heard that I was a Mennonite revivalist, and

Professor Badru Kateregga and me reminiscing on our jointly written book: *A Muslim and a Christian in Dialogue*, at Kampala University, Uganda, 2018.

so they even invited revivalists to join for the Christian gathering. The revivalists greet one another with, "May the Lord be praised," so at the end of the service we greeted one another with those words.

Our host said that it is most unusual for a Muslim and a Christian to embrace such a deep relationship for so many years, and that is why this event with the Muslim and the Christian community in Kampala was so important, for Kampala had known a lot of interreligious strife.

Both Christians and Muslims have had martyrs. Sadly, Uganda has had a history of interreligious conflict with martyrs from all sides. One area in Uganda was Muslim, another area was Catholic, and yet another area was Protestant, with a chieftainship in each section. During our time there, Kateregga took us to the shrine of Muslims killed for their faith. His beautiful land had experienced the suffering of martyrdom.

It is for this reason the streets of Kampala were festooned with banners for our visit, for we two friends embodied a commitment to interfaith peacemaking which was so essential to healing Uganda's past wounds.

Badru told me after the event, "I hope your son Jonathan enjoyed this special arrangement." I was somehow overwhelmed by the gracious concern that we would feel truly at home in this gathering for peace and understanding in Kampala. It was, indeed, a special demonstration of hospitality.

It was a time I will not soon forget.

ETHIOPIA

Ethiopia has a strong engagement with the Ethiopian Coptic Orthodox Church, and Islam bears significant influence within the country as well. During World War II, Ethiopians suffered much, and the Mennonites came forward to do philanthropic work. When the first Mennonite team arrived the government informed them that they could do philanthropic work but no evangelism.

The Mennonites began a high school in Nazareth and some students attended in order to study English. First they used the gospel of John as their textbook with missionary Rohrer Eshleman leading them. Later on they studied the book of Acts. Some students emulated the all-night prayer meetings described in Acts, and as they prayed, God's spirit was poured out, much as we see in Acts 2:17, "I will pour out my Spirit on all people."

When the revival in Ethiopia began in 1964, the total membership in the church was about seven thousand, but soon the Holy Spirit brought conviction and many believed. Students and faculty began to plan for the evangelization of the whole Ethiopian nation. Their strategy became having high school students at the Christian schools enroll in the universities to become teachers. Upon graduation the government assigned placements for these students all across the nation. Then these teachers became the evangelists, teaching and preaching the gospel from one region to another all across Ethiopia. The government gave the teachers their salary.

When we first began traveling to Ethiopia around 1990, I became aware that the walls that separated Muslims and Christians made it quite difficult to develop helpful relationships. In one class that I taught in Addis Ababa, students were asked to go to their Muslim neighbors and ask for suggestions on ways that Christians and Muslims could develop good relationships. My students were very concerned about the assignment—they said that these are the kind of conversations they have not been able to develop effectively.

I asked them to try it anyway, and by the end of the course, the students thanked me for the assignment and said their Muslim neighbors were very grateful for the opportunity to talk with Christians about good neighborliness.

I heard stories of pastors and evangelists from Addis Ababa going three hundred miles north, crossing the rivers into the forest leading into the Wollega region who asked Muslims to carry Bibles across the rivers in waterproof sacks into the communities where Christ was not yet known. As I experienced their fervor it was clear to me that there are three principles that are important as we embark on this type of endeavor: prayer, plan, and partnership.

In another area of Wollega, I went to the great tree in the center of the town and spoke to a hundred children. This is an area where ten years before it had been illegal to preach the gospel. Yet, somehow, there I was, standing under a tree and proclaiming to the children, "Jesus loves you and He wants you to believe in Him." And with one voice all these children proclaimed, "We do love Jesus."

That night we walked through the forest to the village, and I was overcome by the singing of that whole village who had just recently met Jesus. The sound of it was wonderful beyond description! On that trip I asked them how they are progressing with their goals, and they replied that they are praising God because their goal of reaching every people group in Ethiopia with the gospel has been fulfilled. Now they are seeking to enter open doors in regions beyond Ethiopia, such as Sudan.

During the years when the Meserete Kristos Church was illegal and underground, the leadership developed a very comprehensive discipleship training program, and every new believer was expected to enroll in that program. It was an enormous undertaking, but they did it because they were concerned that newborn Christians needed systematic, planned, biblically-grounded equipping in discipleship.

I was in Addis Ababa in 1990, the first time the congregations began to worship above ground. They told me their singing was not yet good, but nevertheless the joy of singing with brothers and sisters after seven years of no audible singing was remarkable. As we left the church center I asked them what message they have for the church in America.

They responded, "Exalt Jesus. That is the message for the church."

With humility and thanksgiving, the Meserete Kristos Church prays that they may become a movement for Jesus, touching peoples with the gospel in Ethiopia and beyond, with special emphasis on the Ethiopian diaspora.

INDONESIA

We witnessed over the years in Ethiopia how, when revival comes, spiritual energies are turned outward in mission, so it was very exciting when this very thing happened in Indonesia.

In the 1960s Indonesians experienced powerful movements of God's spirit, with many young people coming to faith. Indonesian Mennonite leaders decided to begin outreach in mission out of their thankfulness for salvation in Christ. They formed a mission board, PIPKA, that served very much in the same way as Eastern Mennonite Missions. As the mission of PIPKA developed, the leadership believed that fruitfulness requires bridgebuilding with Muslim communities. This led, in Indonesia, to a double engagement in mission: inviting faith in Christ and building peace between Muslims and Christians.

In a variety of ways both Muslim and Christian leaders in Indonesia work at peacebuilding, but I have seen them move

Paulus Hartono, along with me, presenting to an officer *A Muslim and a Christian in Dialogue*, 2007.

beyond simply bridgebuilding to developing helpful relationships and even working on development projects together. They call this the dialogue of praxes. When I asked one of the leaders how he accounts for the growing spirit of peacemaking within Indonesia, this peacemaking pastor said: lots of cups of tea. He described peacemaking as a tea-drinking enterprise touched with the Holy Spirit.

On one of my visits I was invited, along with the local pastor, to join in the breaking of the fast at the end of the Islamic month of Ramadan in Solo, Indonesia. As we were sitting on the floor enjoying dates and tea, I was asked what I am doing to bring peace between Muslims and Christians. I mentioned that one of the things I do is write books to encourage peacemaking and understanding. I presented the book *A Muslim and a Christian in Dialogue*, by myself and

Badru Kateregga. After paging through the book they discussed the possibility of translating it into the local language. A couple years later we were invited for the launching of *A Muslim and a Christian in Dialogue*. That was a marvelous day, seeing Muslims and Christians eating together and the militia commander ordering fifty copies so each of his officers would have one of their own. Now translated into Indonesian, this book is a helpful tool in bridgebuilding.

IRAN

The Bright Future Institute in Tehran convened an event for clerics in September 2006. I wrote to the planners for the Bright Future event and asked if I could do a presentation on Abrahamic Faith, because I saw there was an opening for non-Muslims. The planners welcomed me coming and covered my costs. They told me four thousand clerics would be there from all around the world.

I built my presentation around Luke 4, where Jesus proclaims that today the Messiah is at hand and his reign brings forth peace wherever he is received. I had twenty minutes and concluded by quoting the Lord's Prayer, "Thy Kingdom come, thy will be done on earth as it is in heaven." Quickly I got my earphones, and I heard the cleric who was chairing the meeting. This is what he said: "We did not know this about Jesus. We must investigate, and we need you Christians to make your Scriptures available to us."

I had an opportunity to speak briefly with President Mahmoud Ahmadinejad and I thanked him for the letter that he had written to George Bush, who was the U.S. president at that time. In the letter he urged George Bush to join with him in exploring their respective scriptures and the message of the prophets. After that brief meeting several Anabaptists met with the president of Iran for further conversations. I was not the only voice encouraging conversation; others did as well.

On that trip to Iran I also had an opportunity to meet church leadership. They said, "We cannot exaggerate the significance of what you are doing. You are helping to create space for the church."

Despite much joy and fruitfulness through the years, I also experienced challenges, like in Iran where on another occasion Anabaptists and Muslims were engaged in dialogue. One of the clerics said, "Professor Shenk, why do you always talk about the cross of Christ when you are engaged in dialogue on peacemaking? If you deny the cross of Christ, the door is wide open for Muslims and Mennonites to converge."

I responded, "Jesus crucified and risen is the heart of the gospel. Let me tell a story to explain." Following is the story I told the cleric.

I was in Khartoum, Sudan, preaching to a congregation of mostly widows and orphans. This was my sermon:

> God in Christ is with you in your suffering. His name is Jesus, who was beaten and crucified, who was born among the thorn bushes, who became a refugee, was put on a cross, and as he died proclaimed forgiveness for our sins. In his resurrection, he empowers all who believe to receive forgiveness and extend forgiveness.
>
> So you are not alone.
>
> In Jesus, God is with you, offering a healing grace for you and your families.

After that sermon all these women went into the courtyard and began singing praises to Jesus in whom they are triumphant over all the evil that has been so destructive. These women sang and danced for half an hour—they were dancing because of the love and compassion of Jesus. These women in their sorrows and injustices were experiencing hope in Jesus, our resurrected Savior.

That is why the cross is so central to the gospel. It is in the cross where we meet the Messiah who suffers with us and for us, and that is healing for the person and the nations. We see this in Khartoum, where justice and reconciliation go hand in hand. Widows are being served. Schools are being built for the children. Food is being distributed to the hungry. Our world desperately needs witnesses who proclaim the forgiveness and grace of Christ within our broken world.

17

Six Persons of Peace

In Luke 10, Jesus commanded his disciples to find the person of peace as they go from place to place proclaiming the presence of the kingdom of God. This is why, when I arrive somewhere and leaders say they want to do peace seminars, the first thing I ask is, "Who are the people of peace you are in touch with?"

You can't work at peacemaking if you don't have people of peace (six such persons are listed in this chapter with their names in bold).

I experienced this firsthand when I was introduced to **Professor Badru D. Kateregga** at Kenyatta University College (now Kenyatta University). This is the same Kateregga I have spoken of in previous chapters. He was a Ugandan refugee seeking escape from the atrocities of Idi Amin, and this is when we first met. The two of us had acquired employment as university professors in Kenya in 1973.

He was a devout Sunni Muslim, and I was a Christian, yet we developed an appreciation for one another because both of us enjoyed thinking of new possibilities for communicating the essence of Islam and the Christian faith within the East African context. Within a year we were good friends. Out of that friendship we wrote the book I've spoken of, *A Muslim and a Christian in Dialogue.*

In the first half of the book I confess my faith in Christ and he responds as a Muslim. In the second half of the book Badru confesses his Muslim faith and I respond. This book is now translated into thirteen languages. This book does not criticize, but speaks with gracious critique and includes questions for understanding. Working with Badru on this book was one of the greatest peacemaking exercises of my entire life.

The Arabic translation of this book has been well received in the Middle East and has helped to open doors for dialogue between Muslims and Christians that are quite remarkable. Especially significant is that Badru and I became good friends, and that friendship has enabled the publication of the *Dialogue* in Arabic and other languages as well. This book has encouraged me to bear witness to Jesus with gentle boldness; I think the same could be said of Kateregga in regard to his Muslim faith.

Both Kateregga and I are internationalists and professors. I often hold up the *Dialogue* when I am giving an address, and I say that this *Dialogue* means that we are in competition. Badru builds Muslim universities. I also have been engaged in developing Christian centers of higher learning. Yet even though we are in competition, we cherish our friendship.

Both Muslims and Christians attempt to faithfully proclaim the will of God. For Muslims, God's revelation is centered in the Qur'an; for the Christian, God's full revelation is revealed in Jesus. So our relationships in Christian-Muslim dialogue really have those two different centers. In Islam Jesus is the Messiah, but the Muslim understanding is different than the Christian understanding.

The great question is "How much does God love?" In Islam, God sends his will down because he is merciful. In the Christian faith, God so loves us that God came and lived among us in Jesus the Messiah. That's the question. One night in a Philadelphia mosque the imam said, "Shenk, it is impossible for God to love that much."

And I pled with him, "Let God surprise you."

Another person of peace who has formed me is **Ahmed Ali Haile**. He became a Christian through reading the Bible and was persuaded that in the crucifixion of Jesus we are reconciled

Ahmed Ali Haile—a valiant Somali peacemaker in the way of Christ. A friend who urged David to be a faithful emissary of Jesus Christ, c. 2010.

to God and to one another. He invested much in working for peace between the Somali clans, and during that quest he was hit by a mortar and lost his leg. Although he nearly died, he returned to Somalia and to Kenya working as an interclan peacemaker. He died of cancer, and right up to his death he persisted boldly in calling for all to receive the gift of reconciliation with God and with one another. His book is *Teatime in Mogadishu: My Journey as a Peace Ambassador in the World of Islam.* That book has been translated into other languages and in some areas has caused considerable discussion among the Muslim community.

Other peacemakers often work together in a team. One such team is **Dian Nafi** and **Paulus Hartono**, who worked together

Dian Nafi receiving copies of the *Dialogue* for use in his Muslim leadership training program in Solo, Indonesia, 2007.

as a Muslim and Christian team to develop bridges for peace in sometimes seriously violent situations in Indonesia. Of special concern was the Muslim militia in Central Java, so Paulus climbed the hill to the home of the militia commander. When the commander met the pastor he threatened him; however, the pastor requested a cup of tea. For two years the pastor returned every week for tea with the Muslim militia commander.

This pastor and imam, along with their communities, chartered a plane to Banda Aceh after the tsunami in Indonesia in 2014, and they worked together side by side for two weeks to construct a building that had been destroyed, becoming friends in the process.

Earlier we shared the story about how a Muslim-Christian peace team translated and published *A Muslim and a Christian in Dialogue* into Indonesian. On the day the book was to be launched, the commander along with his soldiers and the pastors met at the Muslim jihadist center to distribute copies of the *Dialogue*. The commander wept, touched by the love he experienced. He asked for fifty copies of the *Dialogue* so that every militia leader could have a copy. He exclaimed that the spirit of the *Dialogue* would change people for good, encouraging them to live peacefully.

Another person of peace told me **he was responsible for arranging the 2005 Bali bombings** in Indonesia. Yet he saw many deaths with no peace. He thought that jihad would bring peace, but even after he had killed so many "infidels," strife continued. In his depression he saw Jesus standing by him and proclaiming that he is the peace. The revelation was of the wounded Messiah, and so he knew that the one who met him was Jesus who was crucified. He is now going to jihadist training centers in Java sharing this message of peace, telling the militia that their bombings are not making peace, only more violence. He tells them that the Prince of Peace appeared to him, and that he is Jesus. He now invites the jihadists to leave their violent ways to follow Jesus who is known as the Prince of Peace.

Women are often especially effective peacemakers. This is the account of a woman who has been a parliamentarian in Somalia named **Fatuma Hashi**, well known for her gentle peacemaking.

Here is her counsel.

My father was a well-known and respectful peacemaking person who earned the nickname of Omar the peacemaker, or "Nabad-doon." I grew up in a home where seeking peace respectfully was an expectation whether in the reading room and library, cultivating good relations with neighbors, or valuing friendship and acting humbly. These were the rules, and my father has been the role model for our extended family. I was successful in my attempts at peacemaking when the individuals or groups were humble, understood the value of forgiveness, will to compromise and respect each other. Some of my strategies were to bring the groups in conflict together and have them discuss their issues and for me just to listen to them and then share some stories about peace. When I would encounter an issue related to a key religious misunderstanding, I would invite a Muslim imam or a Christian pastor to clarify the issue since communities would most likely respect or accept their views more than a person who is not a religious leader. It has been important for me to work with the religious leaders. As a peace clan leader within the Somali context, I remember 'Blessed are the peacemakers for they shall be called the children of God.'

By God's grace, our Shenk family were also emissaries of Jesus and his peace. In fact, the Eastleigh Fellowship Center where we lived was a peacemaking service where Muslims and Christians maintained respectful relationships. The Eastleigh Fellowship Center was recognized as a place of peace. This was an example of the salt and light that Jesus called the light of the world and that light continues to the present time.

18

The Quest for Paradise

In this chapter I want to share about a conversation in a mosque in Philadelphia, Pennsylvania, about the question of what happens when we depart this life. I want to open this conversation with the Fatiha, the opening prayer of the Qur'an.

1. *In the name of God, most Gracious, Most Merciful.*
2. *Praise be to God, the Cherisher and Sustainer of the Worlds;*
3. *Most Gracious, Most Merciful;*
4. *Master of the Day of Judgment.*
5. *You do we worship, and Your aid do we seek.*
6. *Show us the straight way.*
7. *The way of those on whom You have bestowed your grace, those whose (portion) is not wrath, and who do not go astray.*

This prayer is the Fatiha or the opening prayer of the Qur'an, beseeching God to preserve the worshiper from hell and reward the worshiper with paradise. This is the central prayer of the Muslim, the avoidance of final judgment and the reward of eternal paradise. Muslims pray this prayer five times daily facing Mecca. It takes about an hour daily to repeat this prayer in the ritually proper way.

This issue of paradise, as brought up in the Fatiha, came front and center for me during a visit to the Susquehanna mosque in Philadelphia. I enjoyed the professional dynamism of that particular congregation, meeting in the shadow of Temple University with Muslim students working on their doctorates. I know that this mosque touched the global Muslim community, and we met with the imam a couple days before to ask for an invitation to meet.

When we arrived, the mosque was filled. It was Ramadan, the month Muslims believe portions of the Qur'an were first revealed. The participants were both Muslim and Christian.

The imam had flown in to Philadelphia from the United Kingdom for a special time of precise rendition of the Qur'an, so the evening we were there was one of devotees reciting the Qur'an in true Arabic. The cadences and rhythms were beautiful, so foreign to the sounds we might normally hear in a Christian church. Then the imam spoke about the "Night of Power" that Muslims believe is far more excellent than ten thousand nights because this is the night when the Qur'an descended through the agency of the Angel Gabriel. The chanting extended until ten in the evening.

Then those who needed to leave were dismissed while we Christians were seated on the floor to the eastern side of the mosque with the Muslims facing the Christians in a semicircle to facilitate conversation. There were about fifty Christians and one hundred Muslims.

The imam welcomed the guests from London as well as the Christian guests from Philadelphia. He explained that as a special gift the congregation was blessed this Ramadan to have with us persons who read the Qur'an in its beauty.

Then he explained that we make mistakes in life and for that reason the congregation was meeting with their brothers from the UK who were leading the prayers in flawless Arabic, which according to Islam is the language God commands for perfect worship. The Arabic chant, the faithful repetition of the prayers, and good deeds give them hope to acquire paradise.

The imam went on to say that God will notice their extra prayers and expense of coming so far for requesting forgiveness.

In Islam there are scales where the good things you do go on one side and the bad things go on the other side. And for a lifetime a Muslim's primary concern is accumulating credit on the good side of the scales in order to enter paradise. That is the purpose in life: doing enough good things to acquire paradise.

Then I asked, "Have you said enough prayers?

The question elicited silence, then the imam answered, "We have no idea. God is sovereign. There is a balance scales in heaven weighing the good side of the scales. An angel records those good deeds. If a person has committed wrongful deeds an angel likewise will record what he has done. No one knows which side of the ledger is most heavy—the bad or the good."

Then I asked, "May I share with you what the gospel of Jesus the Messiah says about this?"

"Welcome!' the imam exclaimed.

I continued, "Suppose one from among us would commit adultery. How many prayers are needed to deserve forgiveness? We read in the gospel that in Jesus the Messiah God has forgiven our sins and taken them away. God has given Jesus that authority. So with humility and joy we bear witness that our sins are gone when we truly repent!"

"Oh no!" the imam interjected. "If a man has gone to court and is guilty no one can take his place. Only the guilty one can bear the punishment of the wrongdoing."

I responded, "You are right, unless the judge pronounces judgment and then enters the center of the courtroom and takes the place of the guilty one. That is what happened when Jesus the Messiah was crucified. He took our place. The judge of the universe has entered the courtroom and has declared, 'I have taken your place.' We receive the gift of forgiveness by confessing our sins to God, repenting of the wrongs we have done and receiving the grace of forgiveness."

"In the Injil," I continued, referring to the Gospels, "Jesus the Messiah is referred to many times as the Lamb of God. And in the religions and cultures around the world there are these sacrificial animals. I believe those sacrificial animals are signs pointing to Jesus who is the Lamb of God. So wherever the church goes it proclaims the good news that in Jesus who is the Lamb of God we are forgiven."

"Since we are forgiven, paradise is promised. He is the way. He is the way to paradise, the way to salvation, the way to live eternally in God's presence. So I don't ask God to reveal the path to me. Rather I give thanks that the path has been revealed. It is Jesus. He is the path."

There was complete silence in the mosque.

Then the imam said, "This is too deep, too deep for tonight."

"Please," I pled, "hear this good news."

As we left, the participants said, "Thank you! Thank you for coming." And the imam invited us to return for further conversation.

The next meeting I had with the imam took place a month later, with a large group of people, and I reminded him of our conversations the month before. We had another fruitful time together, and again they listened to the Christian message that includes assurance of salvation. What was remarkable is that Islam denies the need for salvation and both of these times I referred to the gift of salvation. I sensed an openness and an eager listening.

The conversations encouraged me. How amazing, to live in a world where Christians and Muslims can converse about such things in peace!

But it shouldn't surprise us. The peace of Jesus whispers in every heart.

19

What a Journey

What a life it has been. After so many years of traveling, Grace and I have settled once again in our home county of Lancaster, Pennsylvania, with family and old friends close by. I still travel and teach, as I can and as I am called, but it is this long life in which Jesus gave me a gentle boldness that I find myself thinking over more and more.

Nearly every morning, Grace and I start off our day by singing a song together while Grace plays the piano. There is a quiet peace there with us in those early hours, a peace that makes it a little bit hard to believe we have traveled all over the world, seen the things we've seen, and known the people who have so changed our lives.

But it's beautiful too, in our house, in the morning light, as we sing together.

> I owe the Lord a morning song
> Of gratitude and praise,

For the kind mercy he has shown
In length'ning out my days.

He kept me safe another night;
I see another day;
Now may his Spirit, as the light,
Direct me in his way.

Keep me from danger and from sin;
Help me thy will to do,
So that my heart be pure within,
And I thy goodness know.

Keep me till thou wilt call me hence,
Where never night can be;
And save me, Lord, for Jesus' sake—
He shed his blood for me.

Often, when I was a boy, my father would sing. He would tell us all to quiet down, and as we grew silent he would listen at the door to see if anyone was coming. There was great opposition in those early days. When all was quiet, Dad would lead us in "Great is Thy Faithfulness," and I could sense the peace of Jesus there with us.

A couple of months ago, I stepped into our dining room where we keep some of the books that I've written. *Look at all of those books*, I thought. Grace and I have been in this together. We are, and always have been, a team, and I often think I never could have imagined what this marriage would be like, but it has been amazing. Her mother told Grace, when she was a twelve-year-old girl washing the windows, "If Jesus calls, say yes."

And she is committed to that call.

Without a wife like Grace, the number of books I wrote would have been greatly reduced. She always stood there with me, and whenever I considered starting a new book, she would affirm it.

And to think this incredible life we have been blessed to spend together all goes back to a Scrabble board along the Millstream, and a winning word:

Joy.

This story of ours began in a little village in central Tanzania, an obscure place called Bumangi, in a community unaware of the possibility of hope. In this journey together we have been energized and encouraged by a hope whose fruit is peace.

I didn't go to bed that night as a child in Mugango planning to meet or hear from Jesus—I was planning to go to sleep. But he called out to me, and I answered, "Yes, Jesus," first asking my parents how to receive him, and then sitting on that bench in our tiny church, contemplating the call. Why he chose me for the mission of my life, I have no idea, but I know I have been under his call, from that point until now. What amazes me is that Jesus chooses such ordinary people. So I join the apostle Paul in his astonishment at having been called, and I say: Thank you.

My sail was set at an early age, not because of my desire, but because of his call. What a privilege. What an honor. As long as I can, I want to walk in fellowship with Jesus.

What comes next?

In the midst of that question, we are touched anew with the hope of Jesus, with whom Grace and I began this journey. We see that the destiny is the fulfillment of God's grand plan to bring to completion the wonderful city he has invited us to build with him, the local and global church.

The singing of the widows and the orphans in Khartoum portrays joyous hope in the midst of calamity, and we have experienced that theme and reality again and again as we have listened to stories of God bringing forth his kingdom. In our churches every Sunday we pray a prayer that Jesus taught the disciples to pray, and we would do well to continue walking with Jesus in his commitment to bringing about his kingdom.

What should we, as followers and proclaimers of the peace of Jesus, do?

The calling of disciples of Jesus is to participate in the healing of the nations. A couple years ago, when I was in Iran with a couple thousand Iranian clerics, they were talking about the quest for hope in their Shi'ite religion. When they asked me to comment, I said that Jesus is our hope, for he is coming again to fulfill the kingdom of God on earth as it is in heaven, so we pray, "Lord, may your kingdom come, your will be done."

At the conclusion of my presentation there, the ayatollah who was moderating the meeting said, "We didn't know this about Jesus. We must investigate, and you Christians must share your books with us so we can read what Shenk is describing."

Let us walk with Jesus as He brings to fulfillment his kingdom.

What we experienced in East Africa some years ago as we began this journey is being fulfilled as people respond to Jesus and walk in his hope.

It has been a joy for me to share the story of the variety of churches whose roots go back deeply into the sixteenth century of the Anabaptist movement. Now as we bring closure to this particular account, I want to look at a biblical passage to give us a biblical, theological foundation as we consider what the next steps before us should be.

Revelation 5 and 6 is a passage of Scripture which describes God's grand plan for history. We are living in tumultuous times, which are in some ways quite similar to those experienced by the early church when these chapters of Revelation were revealed. In Revelation 5 the church is created, and Revelation 6 is the context in which we live. Let us listen to the apostle John as he shares God's revelation about the destiny of history.

John is imprisoned on the island of Patmos by those who opposed the gospel, and he sees God on his throne in heaven. There is a sealed scroll in God's hand; that scroll is the history of humankind. And the question is, "Who is able to unlock that scroll and bring life instead of destruction and death?" The scroll is written on the back side and the front side. The back side would be the history of the past and the front side would be what is happening to our souls right now.

God sends forth messengers seeking for the one who is worthy to open the scroll, the one who is able to deal with our broken, sinful ways. These messengers are looking on the earth, among the places where we do our ideologies and places of business. They look in the realm of the ancestors and no one is found. That search is a metaphor of the quest to find meaning in life, purpose, a worthy destiny.

And no one is found worthy.

So John begins to weep. Not calm, gentle tears. No, great sobbing, an intense weeping. The whole universe is weeping for no one is worthy to bring history to its proper destination.

Suddenly a great angel appears and he calls to John, "Dry your tears, for the person who is worthy has been found to unlock the mystery of the meaning of history." John looks into heaven and he sees Jesus crucified and risen in the center of the throne of God in heaven, and he is given a scroll, for he is worthy to unlock the mystery. He is the Son promised at the dawn of human history. When Adam and Eve turned away from God, God promised that a son born to Adam and Eve would triumph over our sinfulness.

So the promise of a savior begins right at the beginning of human history. God has a plan.

Then God speaks, "The Messiah, Jesus, is worthy to take the scroll because he was slain and, with his blood he purchased humankind for God from every tribe and language and people and nation."

This Jesus, and what he did on the cross and through the resurrection, has redeemed us from the sin of Adam and from the sin of the whole world. And more than that, these redeemed people in verse 10 of Revelation 5 will reign on the earth. The last chapter of the Bible says, "for ever and ever."

That's the plan.

Jesus, and his peace, is the plan.

This Jesus who is the Lamb slain, crucified, resurrected, he is able to create the church, and so God plans to invite ever-widening circles of people into the experience of redemption and forgiveness.

So all of heaven fills with song in Revelation 5:13:

Then I heard every creature in heaven and on earth and under the earth and in the sea, and all that is in them, singing,
"To the one seated on the throne and to the Lamb be blessing and honor and glory and might forever and ever!"

During our many years spent encouraging churches, we were seeking to celebrate the peace of Jesus in the world in which we lived. Jesus commissions us to be his ambassadors of peace. "We are therefore Christ's ambassadors, as though God were making his appeal through us" (2 Corinthians 5:20).

It is through us that God makes his appeal to the world. He calls each of us to go about his business, bringing the peace of Jesus to our homes, our communities, and our nations. What an awesome and exciting invitation!

How will we respond to the call of Christ in our lives?

Epilogue

A dream we had for some years was to plan a safari for our family, including children and grandchildren, enabling all of us to visit eastern Africa that we loved so dearly. That happened some years ago with two separate safari groups. Of course, I was especially eager for each of our grandchildren to visit Bumangi where I had grown up. I couldn't wait to see those old villages and roads through their eyes.

Each safari was about three weeks in duration. We visited game parks, but most importantly we visited the people and places where I had lived as a boy and where later Grace and I raised our family in East Africa. It was also an occasion for the in-laws to meet and greet people and places they had only ever heard about. I cannot express in words what this trip meant to me.

Paul Tournier in his book *A Place For You* writes about needing to find our very special roots by going back home for a visit. That is what happened to our family on these return trips. For me there was added meaning because it was the place where I had first said "Yes" to Jesus.

Of particular interest was returning to our home in Eastleigh, where so many memories waited for us. It was a great joy to see how the seed of hope had grown that was planted some years earlier: a vibrant ministry had prospered there, taking the form of English classes, Bible classes, basketball, reading rooms, a library, and fellowship meetings. A special treat was stopping at a local restaurant for Somali food, including smoked camel milk, which our grandchildren drank zestfully, for the experience. With mixed emotions, we walked through the halls of the home where we had lived.

We visited in the home of Erastus, Agnes, and their children and grandchildren, who had lived in the same apartment building with us in Eastleigh. We prayed, sang, and reminisced together. Also we visited Bishop Joshua Okello and his family, who lived in Eastleigh in the apartment above us.

Shortly after our visit the girls basketball team wrote a letter to me inviting us to sponsor a tournament for girls. Our congregation at Mountville did that and the tournament was a smashing hit all across Nairobi.

Our hosts were delighted that the great-grandchildren of Clyde and Alta Shenk would have come to visit where we had lived and played so many years ago, feasting on goat with them once again. We will remember that visit forever.

We have asked each of our children to share a highlight of our trip to East Africa. Here it is, in their words.

KAREN

Standing on the shoreline of Lake Victoria in Tanzania, in July 2016, with my father and mother, my two daughters ages nine

The Shenk family at the place where Elam and Ruth Stauffer and John and Ruth Mosemann landed on the shores of Lake Victoria, 2016.

and fifteen, and my youngest brother and his family, I was transported back in time, decades prior, as my father told the story of the first Mennonite mission workers who came across the big lake in a fishing dhow, to share Jesus with this community, by the shores of Lake Victoria. As my father was telling the story, there was a gentle breeze blowing across the lake, and there were two fishing dhows within our sights, with fishermen busy casting their nets and catching fish. I tried to imagine a Caucasian male and his luggage coming across the big lake in such a dhow, to bring the gospel of Jesus to this community. It was meaningful for me to stand along Lake Victoria with my father, who was born in Tanzania, and whose entire life was shaped by the Mennonite pioneer mission work in Tanzania. I too was shaped by that mission work in Tanzania, since my father's zeal for missions brought him back to East

The Shenk family at the place where Elam and Ruth Stauffer and John and Ruth Mosemann landed on the shores of Lake Victoria, 2012.

Africa as a young adult with family in tow, which included myself as a two-year-old. I treasure that visit by Lake Victoria and am filled with gratitude for this legacy. I am glad for the photo from that visit of my dad, eldest son of Clyde and Alta, standing with me, eldest daughter of David and Grace, along with a photo of myself with my daughters. I hope parts of this legacy pass on to their generation.

DORIS

On a quiet afternoon in Shirati, we took a short ride to the shores of Lake Victoria. The local pastor, John Wamburu, led us to the one break in the road to access the water. We stepped onto the ledge overlooking the lake—no other docks in sight—as my father and the pastor recounted the first Mennonites arriving to this place. We imagined the young American couple pushing the log poles against the lake bottom to lodge their boat into the muddy shore, hauling their life's belongings onto the rugged land. Here Mennonites and Africans met for the first time, marking the beginning of our unlikely family legacy, straddling two continents, and over many generations. The lake was beautiful, the setting peaceful, and our children, after absorbing the significance of this spot, started clowning around on the edge of the lake, pretending to fall in. What else but giddiness to accompany such amazement.

JONATHAN

As a child growing up in East Africa, I have fond memories of long, uninterrupted hours playing in the outdoors. My son Gabriel grew up on bedtime stories about my childhood in Kenya and Somalia. In fact, when my wife Cynthia and I first mentioned my parents' invitation to travel to East Africa he was initially hesitant: What about the snakes and hyenas, and the jiggers that dig into your toes?

Cynthia had already visited Kenya and Somalia years ago with my family when we were dating. This was Gabriel's first foray—as a fourteen-year-old—and he and I had so much fun exploring the places and meeting the friends from those childhood stories. With our trusty Swahili-English dictionary we encouraged each other to express ourselves in Swahili. We found trees to climb together, local fruit and dishes to enjoy, and neighborhoods to jog through in the early morning hours, including a run through a game park with a Maasai warrior running alongside us for protection from any unsuspecting wild animals.

When Gabriel returned to his cross-country team in New Jersey after several weeks of running in the higher Kenyan altitudes, he had an extra kick in his step. And since Kenyans are well known long-distance running champs—several of them at that time with a variation of "Kip" in their names—Gabriel found he had soon adopted the nickname "Kip" or "Kip Yoder Shenk" among his running friends.

TIMOTHY

One of my highlights was visiting Bumangi, my dad's childhood home. It was my first visit to Bumangi, and I was excited to see the place my dad had talked about so frequently, and to share the experience with my wife and kids. We arrived on a Sunday morning, and we could hear the choir singing long before we got to the church doors since they were using huge loudspeakers. Since the choir was dancing as well as singing, the children sitting on the floor near the front had to scoot back to create enough space. After the service, we went into my dad's childhood home, and the host provided my niece with a live chicken for us to take back to the United States. We respectfully declined the gift, but not before taking plenty of pictures of the family and the chicken in front of my dad's childhood home. We also saw my grandma's clinic, where she dispensed basic medicine to her neighbors. Before leaving, we were treated to a huge feast of rice, vegetables, goat, and chicken. What a day!

It was thrilling to see our children enrich their lives and the lives of others by incorporating their African experiences here.

Their fortitude and resilience showed up in so many ways. We worked with our children to have the funds for them to go to Christian schools from middle school through college. This enabled them to find community and spiritual formation. They continue to be in touch with some of their friends from those days and our sons met their wives in college.

We believe that the challenges they have experienced and their crosscultural lives have specially equipped them for a ministry of compassion and are grateful for the energetic healing and hope ministries that our children are engaged in.

We are delighted by our children and grandchildren. We cheer them on and they cheer us onward.

Karen works as a psychiatric registered nurse at Lancaster Behavioral Health Hospital in Lancaster, Pennsylvania. Karen and Merv have two children, adopted from Guatemala: Dulce and Vanessa. Merv is involved in marketing with Benjamin Roberts.

Doris is a social worker with Bethanna, an agency in Lancaster, involved with the foster care of children. Doris and

Family Picture: David and Grace Shenk's 50th Wedding Anniversary, 2009

First Row, kneeling, left to right: Christine Kaufman, Maia Shenk, Amani Kaufman, Dulce Shenk Zeager, Vanessa Shenk Zeager, Karen Shenk Zeager
Second Row, left to right: Timothy Shenk, Owen Corkery, Merv Zeager
Third Row, left to right: Cynthia Yoder, Doris Shenk
Fourth Row, left to right: Gabriel Yoder Shenk, Jonathan Shenk, David and Grace, Caleb Corkery, Chloe Corkery

Caleb have two children, Chloe and Owen. Caleb is a professor at Millersville University.

Jonathan and Cynthia have a son, Gabriel. Jonathan is owner of Greenleaf Painters, LLC, in Princeton Junction, New Jersey. He is an ordained Presbyterian minister and is involved in criminal justice reform advocacy work. Cynthia works as a business consultant in Jonathan's company and is an author.

Timothy is the community education program director at Lancaster-Lebanon Intermediate Unit 13, an education service agency. Tim and Christine have two children, Amani and Maia. Christine is a behavioral health consultant at the Lancaster Health Center.

Our family's church experience is quite varied, which creates some energetic and meaningful conversations—Mennonite, Presbyterian, and Quaker.

Our children amaze us with their joviality and good humor in the midst of their robust commitments. We enjoy sharing stories with each other when we get together for vacations and holidays. The adults don't usually get around to playing games or watching sports as there is too much to share when we have the opportunity to be together. We are grateful for the family God has given to us.

Acknowledgments

I am an internationalist and have invested much of my life
ministering within eastern Africa. This book describes the
challenges I have experienced living within the international
context for so many years. My focus has been particularly in
peacemaking, and in a very specific way peacemaking between
Christians and Muslims. This ministry has called forth doors of
opportunity which often leave me astonished. So my acknowl-
edgment statement is a brief comment on the various persons
and agencies who have joined with me in the quest to walk in
Christ's way within the pluralistic world in which I live.

My sojourn within the international context has been salted
and informed by the church. Within the hundred countries that
I have served in a variety of ways, the church has been embracing me, welcoming me, and informing me. We thank you for
the hospitality we have experienced in so many settings.

My primary connections have been Tanzania, Somalia, Kenya, and the United States. I have chosen to focus briefly on those four, mostly because those four are where I have been most fully engaged. These four countries lend themselves well to congenial peacemaking within the hospitality-oriented communities of eastern Africa.

My international engagements were first and foremost birthed by my father and mother, who were pioneer Mennonite missionaries in Tanzania in 1936. We had no home leave for ten years, so my early life was deeply formed by Africans. My earliest recollections include statements from my mother when she would say, "How blessed we are to serve among these hospitable people." Living within the African context provided opportunity to be significantly informed by African values and spirituality.

In later years as our ministry in peacemaking expanded, a team emerged under Eastern Mennonite Missions to give counsel and direction for our ministries, particularly as our ministries related to peacemaking. This was the Christian-Muslim Relations Team. Shortly thereafter a small group initiated what became a network of international partners, the Peacemakers Confessing Christ International team. An oversight committee of approximately twelve guided our steps from the beginning of our consultancy work.

Very significantly Kenyatta University offered me a position as lecturer at the university. From that vantage position several books emerged which have been received around the world as a helpful forum for dialogue. The university also endorsed a major study in traditional African peacemaking, involving seventy students. My research enabled me to develop a substantive book on peacemaking in Africa.

In all these engagements it was the church, particularly the Kenya and Tanzania Mennonite churches, who helped to provide me with a sense of authentic rootedness in all these ministries.

This has been a surprising journey and this book in our hands today is the fruit of hundreds of conversations between Muslims and Christians as I seek to find the way of peacemaking in the way of Christ.

My mentor over the years has been Ahmed Ali Haile, a professor at Daystar University, prior to his death. His book *Teatime in Mogadishu* powerfully informed my approaches to peacemaking. He often reminded his Christian fellow travelers that we should never forget that we have been called by Jesus to be his envoys.

Truly I am indebted to so many who have explored the trails, the pathways, that were before us and led us onward in the directions those paths would take us. That is what this book is all about. The ministry is reaching out in a variety of ways that we don't perceive yet.

Eastern Mennonite Missions has carried forward this project with gracious commitment. Jerry Keener, former president, applauded the vision along with the vice president, Joe Hollinger. Shawn Smucker, our collaborator, has brought expertise and commitment to the table. Herald Press has published several of my books, which is enormously appreciated. The Lancaster Conference Historical Society has provided archival expertise. They have been helpful.

This book has been a four-year conversation, usually between Grace and me, as the chapters have unfolded. It is her enthusiasm and loving presence that have made this memoir possible. Her dynamic participation has made this book a joy, for it has been a forum of remembrances. We have been a team working together. This book is a highlight for me. It has been wonderful working together with Grace in this commitment.

We acknowledge the festive engagement of our children and grandchildren in developing these memoirs. Their wise counsel and suggestions were so helpful. They are also a part of the journey.

I am grateful for all who have so richly welcomed me to serve locally and internationally. May God be praised.

My Life Commitment

David W. Shenk

My life commitment is:

- To grow in knowing and loving Jesus Christ through the faithful reading of his Word, prayer, daily repentance, and in open fellowship with the Holy Spirit and the church.
- To glorify Christ by prayerfully and faithfully fulfilling his anointing on me to be a faithful husband, father, and grandfather.
- To invest my life in the ministry of the gospel as I give witness to Christ our savior wherever I go or live, in obedience to the leading of the Holy Spirit.
- To encourage, equip, and enable others to serve in the world harvest, especially among those who have never heard of Christ.

Appendix I

The Revival in East Africa

Those among us who want to know dates and places will probably trace the beginnings of the revival to a high school teacher in Rwanda, Blasio Kigozi, in the mid-1930s, who invested twelve days in prayer and fasting for the out-pouring of the Holy Spirit upon the students, staff, and faculty.

Blasio came from his room, a transformed man, first asking his wife and family for forgiveness for his wrongful attitude and then convening a meeting of all faculty and staff to announce that the Lord had revealed the need for repentance. The whole school was convicted. The Anglican bishops in Kampala invited Blasio to meet with the bishops and they also were touched with a deep need for repentance. Within six weeks Blasio took ill and died.

However, Blasio's message across East Africa has never ceased. In the convicting power of the Holy Spirit the

Mennonites were not passed by, for the convicting power of the Holy Spirit moved across the Mennonite areas. In various ways all the countries of eastern Africa were touched by the revival that still continues today. The revivalist Christians stayed within their denominations. They did not form new denominations.

Let me comment very briefly on the various fruit of the revival.

1. First, the revival is centered in Jesus Christ. Every fellowship meeting is centered in Jesus.

2. Every fellowship includes the confession of sin and the celebration of the cleansing blood of Jesus. First John 1:7-10 summarizes the central commitments of the Revival Fellowship: "If we walk in the light, as he is in the light, we have fellowship with one another, and the blood of Jesus, his Son, purifies us from all sin. If we claim to be without sin, we deceive ourselves and the truth is not in us. If we confess our sins, he is faithful and just and will forgive us our sins and purify us from all unrighteousness. If we claim we have not sinned, we make him out to be a liar and his word is not in us."

3. The revivalists ministered with fervency. They were nicknamed "the people inflamed with passion for Jesus," thus the name *balokole*. Even today across East Africa the revivalists are known as the balokole, people who are on fire for Jesus.

4. The fellowships are communities of joy. They encompass people from tribes and nations all across East Africa. Acts 2:5-6: "Now there were staying in Jerusalem God-fearing Jews from every nation under

heaven. When they heard this sound, a crowd came together in bewilderment, because each one heard their own language being spoken."

5. The movement became the most authentic intertribal community in East Africa. Their spirit of inter-community relationship was a key development in encouraging peaceful efforts for healing the political strife in Kenya.

6. They also carried the name People of the Lamb. That name came from their martyr stories. Very early on in the movement in Kenya and Uganda, as well as Burundi and Rwanda, there was turmoil from tribal or international conflict. The revivalists refused to participate in these violent conflicts. Hundreds died bearing witness that Jesus is the Lamb of God. They laid down their lives for Jesus. They were called the People of the Lamb because they were peacemakers.

7. Several times in Kenya's tumultuous postindependence history, the Mennonites have stood boldly with the People of the Lamb, declaring that they are committed to the healing of the nations, not the destruction of the nations. In some of these political circumstances it is the churches who joined hands to preserve the peace of the nations.

There is a song concerning Jesus and his shed blood which over the years became the anthem for the revival, "Utukufu Alleluia" ("Praise the Lord, Hallelujah").

Several spiritual streams have joined together within the revival fellowship. First is John Bunyan and his *Pilgrims Progress*. Second would be a spirituality akin to the Wesleyan Methodist. The third stream is authentically African. The revival has been an African movement wherein Jesus is paramount. The fourth stream would be akin to the Anabaptist movement.

The revivalists are recognized as a fellowship who love Jesus, lighting a thousand lights as they meet daily for worship and prayers.

One of the joyous consequences for the Mennonites of the revival was the ordination of the first four Mennonite pastors in 1950 on two occasions: Ezekiel K. Muganda, Andrea M. Mabeba, Zedekia M. Kisare, and Nashon K. Nyambok. The region became a festival of joy as people gathered from far and wide to celebrate that God had provided four pastors for the Tanzania Mennonite Church.

Appendix II

Anthropology, Writings, and Agency Partners

I have been extremely blessed in the opportunities to write that have come to me through the years.

In 1972, when we were on home leave from Somalia, I completed my PhD program. When people asked, during our home leave, when we would be returning to Somalia, one of our children said, "When we complete Dad's dissertation." We were all in it together. This goes to show how much of a family effort my education had become.

The physical creation of it involved a lot of cutting and pasting, as the document had to be rearranged before the days of computers. It was a delightful study about "Mennonite Presence and Church Development in Somalia."

Prior to concluding my dissertation, I wrote my first book, *Mennonite Safari,* the story of Mennonite presence in Tanzania. Subsequently I wrote a substantial book on world religions, entitled *Global Gods,* which was an open door for me into the world of universities. This book explores the world of religions in modern societies, written from a shalom focus. How can religions contribute to more of a shalom focus? In my teaching of world religions, I look at the three questions every society asks: Why am I here? How can I find forgiveness? What is my destiny? Then I teach what each religion says about these three questions. My text helps a shalom focus to emerge.

This construct is now available for students, and I'm told that Vilnius University in Lithuania is now using it as a textbook. It has been translated into the Lithuanian language. I was surprised and grateful that this text has been used in post-Marxist universities.

Another contribution is a study of peacemaking, and I would ask my religious studies class at Kenyatta University in Nairobi, Kenya, to interview their grandparents to discover ways traditional society developed commitments to peacemaking. I was surprised to learn that all traditional societies formed a covenant that was sealed in the sacrificial blood of an innocent victim. As an anthropologist this is exceedingly significant.

As I listened to my African Christian colleagues at the university, I learned that they viewed the animal sacrifices within their traditional religion as signs pointing to the universal truth of Jesus, the Lamb of God. In the traditional system the animal sacrifice is viewed as an innocent victim who absorbs the violence and breaks the cycle of violence; for the sacrifice does not take vengeance, it absorbs the violence but does not perpetuate the violence. When we focus on Jesus who does not perpetuate the violence, we see open arms who invite reconciliation, not vengeance. So in the Christian understanding, God in Jesus with open arms invites protagonists to come and experience his peace and forgiveness. The tribal religions are a sign in traditional African religion pointing to Jesus who is the ultimate sacrifice. He is the Lamb of God.

When we look at this from a biblical commitment, we meet the perfect Lamb who is the peace offering. In Jesus we have met the one who is the eternal seal of the covenant peace offering. All of these sacrifices are signs pointing to the Lamb who is sacrificed from the foundation of the world, the Lamb standing in the center of the throne (Revelation 5:6). My book *Justice, Reconciliation and Peace in Africa* speaks to those issues.

Over the years I have authored or coauthored twenty books related to themes that I want to address in regard to Christian and Muslim relations and Jesus in a world of pluralism. This morning I received a letter from a university professor who says my approach to African traditional religion, viewing the faith as preparation for the gospel, transformed his teaching some twenty years ago. That kind of letter is why I write!

An exciting development was an invitation extended by the Ministry of Education, to me and my Catholic colleague at Kenyatta University, to write a history of the early church in Africa. Several African educationalists wanted to see the history available in the curriculum for senior high school students. Many Africans assumed that the Christian faith was a Western faith and they needed something from the African context. The Catholic scholar was John Kealy and I was the Protestant scholar. History is one of my areas of expertise. Students and faculty across the continent were very keen about having a history of Christianity available. It was a joy to work with the Catholic church and Orthodox and Protestants in making available to them the story of non-Western texts. That was an exhilarating assignment and was appreciated in the academic world. The name of the book is *The Early Church and Africa*.

My work as an administrator for international missions with EMM was also encouraging. I was deeply grateful for the emergence of new conferences of churches. To the glory of God I was awarded two alumni awards of the year for exemplifying Christlike love, peacemaking, and service. In 2003 I was given the Distinguished Service Award from Eastern Mennonite University and in 2007 I was given the Alumnus of the Year Award from Lancaster Mennonite School, may God be praised.

EMM and its partners planted both home and international churches during my service there. I served for seven and a half years in home ministries and eleven years in the international departments of EMM. I enjoyed my perch for EMM-related ministries. I also enjoyed the interrelationships with organizations such as Mennonite Central Committee and Mennonite Mission Network. I experienced much joy relating to the global church. A special privilege for me was a monthly lunch with Ray Brubacher, director of international programs for MCC. Those were quiet conversations. Then there were the energizing times with the many internationals who came through our offices. My recollections of the connections with the frontiers of mission and service around the world are unforgettable and I am deeply grateful for the many ways I experienced affirmation and helpful counsel. We were aware that Orie Miller, who directed MCC for many years, was also the director of Eastern Mennonite Board of Missions and Charities, now EMM. We knew that we should also build upon that legacy of interagency cooperation that was typical of MCC at its beginnings.

EMM was greatly blessed in multiple experiences of MCC and mission boards cooperating together. I think, for example, of the China Educational Exchange program, where the mission agencies and MCC joined hands together in remarkable engagements with Chinese universities, or in the Middle East, where for a period of time three of the agencies had volunteers serving in Israel, Palestine, and Jordan. Much work has been done. Much work remains. May we all say yes to the call of Jesus in our lives. May God be praised.

Appendix III

Organizations and Ongoing Ministry

At the conclusion of one trip to Indonesia, where I was focusing on Christian-Muslim relations within a particularly tragic time in Indonesia because of destructive relationships, the Holy Spirit impressed upon me that this ministry of Christian-Muslim peacemaking needed to expand. Likewise, with clarity on that flight the Lord indicated that Andres Prins and Jonathan Bornman had been equipped to serve with me as partners. I was quite excited, and as soon as I got home I made arrangements to meet with Andres and Jonathan to share the vision. They felt it was God's appointment for them. It was quite remarkable that when we shared this vision with our EMM leadership there was immediate enthusiasm. That was in 2012.

Jonathan Bornman and Andres Prins arrived with exten-
sive experience of service to Christ in Muslim societies of West
Africa and North Africa respectively, and seemed a providen-
tial fit to help carry the load of ministry. We became a team
of five members who among us knew eight languages, all with
international experience with special focus on Islamic ministries. Angie Breneman Earl joined the team, as did Grace. We
became the Christian-Muslim Relations Team (CMRT).

Landing on a team name and description that communi-
cated truthfully to both Muslims and Christians took some
work and time. We prayerfully asked the guidance of the Holy
Spirit to give direction. After about a month we came to a
united conviction: Eastern Mennonite Missions Christian-
Muslim Relations Team, Peacemakers Confessing Christ.
In an attempt to clarify for everyone what we understood
as our Christ-given witness, we drew up a list of commitments to which we invited all who might observe us to hold
us accountable.

In 2013 Peacemakers Confessing Christ International
(PCCI) was conceived during a prayer meeting when the idea
came to create a network of persons who had been shaped
in some way by participants in the CMRT. The network was
birthed at a small gathering of ten persons in Bonn, Germany,
where it was decided to create a monthly prayer letter. Praying
and sharing prayer requests remains a core element of PCCI,
and it continues to operate under CMRT.

While the network is young, its members span the globe.
The network's members' cumulative experience and insight
add up to more than a century of respectful, trust-building
relationships. Their joyful experience of the indwelling transforming work of Jesus motivates them to engage in peacemaking, and the biblical mandate to love God and one's neighbor.

A large part of what the CMRT does is equip others to be involved in peacemaking in the way of Christ. It is important to understand the worldview of the other in order to participate in meaningful interaction. The books which we distribute widely are transformative, for every book in various ways exalts Jesus

EMM's Christian-Muslim Relations Team (CMRT). There is fluidity in the membership. David and Grace are in the back row with appointee Angie Breneman Earl. In the front row are appointees Andres Prins and Jonathan Bornman, 2018.

as the gift of eternal peace to all who believe. Wherever we go
we carry our books, many of which I have authored or coauthored. The four books in the *Christians Meeting Muslims
Series* are: *A Muslim and a Christian in Dialogue, Journeys
of the Muslim Nation and the Christian Church, Teatime in
Mogadishu,* and *Christian. Muslim. Friend.* The one-word
description of each book respectively is: Dialogue, Witness,
Peacemaking, and Hospitality.

Another international congregation I've had the privilege
of being involved with from time to time is the Singapore
Mennonite Church, and occasionally I have taught in their
leadership training ministry, Bethany International University.
I discovered early on that our approaches to evangelism vary
greatly. For example, in Singapore they have a simple philosophy of ministry: each one, teach one. That is the curriculum
for their school of missiology. The graduates of the Bethany
school are scattered around the world, serving with the vision
of "each one, teach one." In a recent trip I taught twenty-six
students from nine nationalities.

One beautiful thing about the community in Singapore is
that it is engaged in lively dialogue with a variety of religious
communities. These experiences of dialogue are equipping
them for trust-building among diverse communities such as
Buddhists, Muslims, or Confucianists. It is quite remarkable
the way these evangelical Christians find open doors to bear
witness to Christ.

Bethany also has a remarkable philosophy when it comes
to finance: No student is to concern himself or herself for
school fees and living expenses. Bethany International University assures students that God will provide for their
finances. Indeed, this is a school made possible by the gifts of
God's people.

It has been a great honor to work with so many wonderful organizations around the world. There are so many people pursuing peace between Muslims and Christians, a fact that gives me great hope.

Appendix IV

Books on Peacemaking

The Call of the Minaret, 2nd edition, Kenneth Cragg, Oxford University Press, 1989

Entertaining Angels Unaware, Philip A. Gottschalk, Cascade, 2021

The Gentle Answer, Gordon Nickel, Bruton Gate, 2015

A Gentle Wind of God, Richard K. MacMaster with Donald R. Jacobs, Herald Press, 2006

Joyful Witness in the Muslim World, Evelyn A. Reisacher, Baker Academic, 2016

Kisare, A Mennonite of Kiseru, as Told to Joseph C. Shenk, Eastern Mennonite Missions, 1984

The Muslim Jesus, Tarif Khalidi, Harvard University Press, 2001

Once We Were Strangers, Shawn Smucker, Revell, 2018

Peace Catalysts, Rick Love, Intervarsity Press, 2014

Peace Clan, Peter M. Sensenig, Wipf and Stock, 2016

Summoned From the Margin, Lamin Sanneh, Eerdmans, 2012

BOOKS AUTHORED OR COAUTHORED BY DAVID SHENK:

Anabaptists Meeting Muslims: A Calling for Presence in the Way of Christ, edited with James Krabill and Linford Stutzman, Herald Press, 2005

Christian. Muslim. Friend., Herald Press, 2014

Creating Communities of the Kingdom, coauthored with Ervin Stutzman, Herald Press, 1998

The Early Church and Africa, coauthored with John Kealy, Oxford University Press, 1976

Global Gods: Exploring the Role of Religions in Modern Societies, 2nd edition, Herald Press, 1998

The Holy Book of God, Evangel Press, 1978

Journeys of the Muslim Nation and the Christian Church: Exploring the Mission of Two Communities, Herald Press, 2003

Justice, Reconciliation and Peace in Africa, Eastern Mennonite Missions, 1997

A Muslim and a Christian in Dialogue, coauthored with Badru Kateregga, Herald Press, 2011

Surprises of the Christian Way, Herald Press, 2000

Teatime in Mogadishu: My Journey as Ambassador of Peace in the World of Islam, by Ahmed Ali Haile, as told to David W. Shenk, Herald Press, 2011

The Author

D avid W. Shenk is the founder emeritus member of the Christian-Muslim Relations Team for Eastern Mennonite Missions. He is a pastor, writer, internationalist, and missions leader. His particular focus is on bearing witness to the peace of Christ in a world of religious and ideological pluralism. He is a professor and author or coauthor of twenty books, including *A Muslim and a Christian in Dialogue*, *Journeys of the Muslim Nation and the Christian Church*, *Teatime in Mogadishu* and *Christian. Muslim. Friend.*